MPRESSIONS of the

NEW FOREST & ISLE OF WIGHT

Produced by AA Publishing

Published by AA Publishing (a trading name of Automobile Association Developments Limited, whose registered office is Fanum House, Basing View, Basingstoke, Hampshire RG21 4EA; registered number 1878835)

ISBN 978-0-7495-5547-4

A03033g

A CIP catalogue record for this book is available from the British Library.

Colour reproduction by KDP, Kingsclere
Printed and bound in China by C&C Offset Co Ltd

Opposite: Setting out on the Round the World Yacht race

IMPRESSIONS of the

NEW FOREST & ISLE OF WIGHT

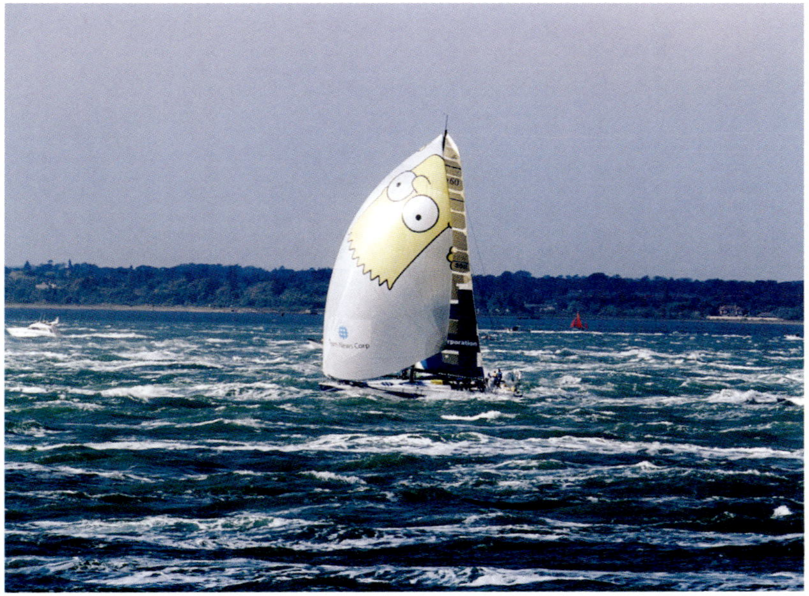

Acknowledgements

The Automobile Association would like to thank the following photographers, companies and picture libraries for their assistance in the preparation of this book.

Abbreviations for the picture credits are as follows – (t) top; (b) bottom; (c) centre; (l) left; (r) right; (AA) AA World Travel Library.

Front cover AA/A Burton; back cover main AA/A Burton; back cover inset AA/S McBride; 3 AA/S McBride; 5 AA/S McBride; 7 AA/A Burton; 8 AA/S&O Matthews; 9 AA/R Fletcher; 10 AA/A Burton; 11 AA/A Burton; 12 AA/A Burton; 13 AA/T Souter; 14 AA/D Forss; 15 AA/A Burton; 16 AA/P Baker; 17 AA/A Burton; 18 AA/A Burton; 19 AA/A Burton; 20 AA/A Burton; 21 AA/A Burton; 22 AA/A Burton; 23 AA/A Burton; 24 AA/S McBride; 25 AA/D Forss; 26 AA/W Voysey; 27 AA/S McBride; 28 AA/S McBride; 29 AA/W Voysey; 30 AA/R Fletcher; 31 AA/AJ Hopkins; 32 AA/A Burton; 33 AA/A Burton; 34 AA/A Burton; 35 AA/A Burton; 36 AA/S McBride; 37 AA/A Burton; 38 AA/A Burton; 39 AA/S McBride; 40 AA/W Voysey; 41 AA/A Burton; 42 AA/A Burton; 43 AA/A Burton; 44 AA/A Burton; 45 AA/A Burton; 46 AA/A Burton; 47 AA/A Burton; 48 AA/A Burton; 49 AA/S McBride; 50 AA/W Voysey; 51 AA/W Voysey; 52 AA/S McBride; 53 AA/S McBride; 54 AA/A Burton; 55 AA/S McBride; 56 AA/A Burton; 57 AA/A Burton; 58 AA/A Burton; 59 AA/A Burton; 60 AA/D Forss; 61 AA/D Forss; 62 AA/A Burton; 63 AA/W Voysey; 64 AA/S McBride; 65 AA/W Voysey; 66 AA/A Burton; 67 AA/A Burton; 68 AA/S&O Matthews; 69 AA/W Voysey; 70 AA/A Burton; 71 AA/A Burton; 72 AA/A Burton; 73 AA/T Souter; 74 AA/A Burton; 75 AA/A Burton; 76 AA/A Burton; 77 AA/A Burton; 78 AA/A Burton; 79 AA/A Burton; 80 AA/R Fletcher; 81 AA/W Voysey; 82 AA/A Burton; 83 AA/A Burton; 84 AA/A Burton; 85 AA/A Burton; 86 AA/A Burton; 87 AA/A Burton; 88 AA/A Burton; 89 AA/A Burton; 90 AA/W Voysey; 91 AA/S McBride; 92 AA/A Burton; 93 AA/A Burton; 94 AA/T Souter; 95 AA/A Burton:

Opposite: View of the Needles craggy rocks and the lighthouse from the white cliffs, Isle of Wight

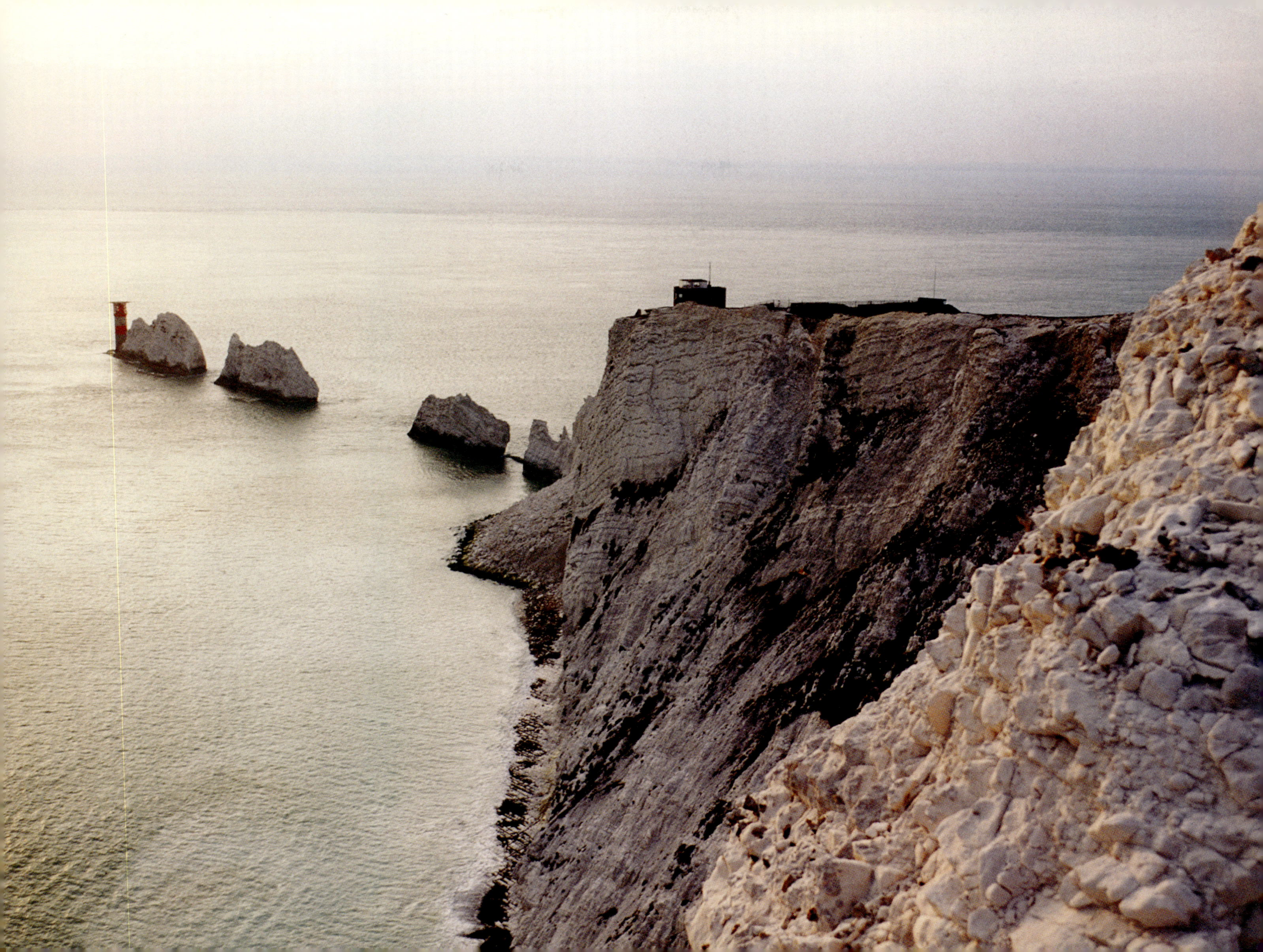

INTRODUCTION

Wild ponies graze while long-legged foals take their first teetering steps, a sparrow hawk hovers, pigs greedily feast on acorns and in the distance echoes the deep, guttural grunt of rutting deer as the autumn deepens, just as they all have done for centuries. These are the architects of the New Forest created in 1079 by William the Conqueror. When William brought the land the beasts of the chase – wild pig and deer – and their food were protected for the pleasure of the monarch. No longer hunted, the deer roam freely. From the majestic red deer to the little sika and the roe and fallow deer with their striped rump and velvet antlers, all are at home in their special preserve.

The New Forest National Park was created in March 2005 to conserve and enhance the natural beauty, wildlife and cultural heritage of the area. It is the eighth national park in England. Covering 150 square miles of wild, beautiful scenery, it lies mainly in south-west Hampshire – from east of the Avon Valley to Southampton Water and from the Solent coast to the edge of the Wiltshire chalk downs. All animals roam freely and have the right of way through the woods, thickets and open heathland. As well as their usual diet of grass, heather, prickly gorse and brambles – for which they have specially adapted horny tongues – they love green acorns. During autumn, pigs are turned out into the Forest for 'pannage' to forage for acorns and so protect the ponies who are poisoned by too many of them. The old oak and beech of the ancient and ornamental woodlands are dressed in all their finery at this time of year, in the russet golden colours of autumn.

In the southernmost part lies Beaulieu and the historic village, Buckler's Hard. Originally an 18th-century port for importing sugar from the West Indies, it evolved into a famous shipbuilding village, using the mighty oaks from the Forest. The splendid *HMS Agamemnon*, in which Nelson was later to lose his right eye, was built here by the most celebrated Master Shipbuilder, Henry Adams, in 1781. Among the New Forest's most celebrated residents were Florence Nightingale and Sir Arthur Conan Doyle, creator of Sherlock Holmes, who lived in Minstead.

From the coast of the New Forest it is only a 30-minute ferry crossing to the Isle of Wight. Lewis Carroll visited Alfred, Lord Tennyson, the Poet Laureate, at his home in Freshwater in 1859, now known as the Tennyson Heritage Coast. Countless visitors share his appreciation of this lovely coastline. Queen Victoria first visited the Island as a princess which was the beginning of her 70-year love affair with the Island. She and Prince Albert moved to the Island in 1864 to Osborne House where she lived until her death. In contemporary times, Dame Ellen MacArthur, the youngest and fastest woman to sail around the world, had her first sailing holiday to the Island at the age of eight and now has a house in the sailing mecca, Cowes.

Over half of the Island is designated as an Area of Outstanding Natural Beauty and, with a network of footpaths stretching over 500 miles, it's easy to get close to nature in a glorious variety of landscape from lush green pastures to rolling downs backed by mineral-rich, high chalk cliffs. Parkhurst is the only forest on the Island which is a haven for wildlife, including a thriving population of red squirrels.

From the Forest wilderness to the sparkling Island, in every season and in every light, this is a true wonderland, over endowed with natural riches.

At Ipley, three miles north of Beaulieu, the Beaulieu River is no more than a small stream this far into the Forest

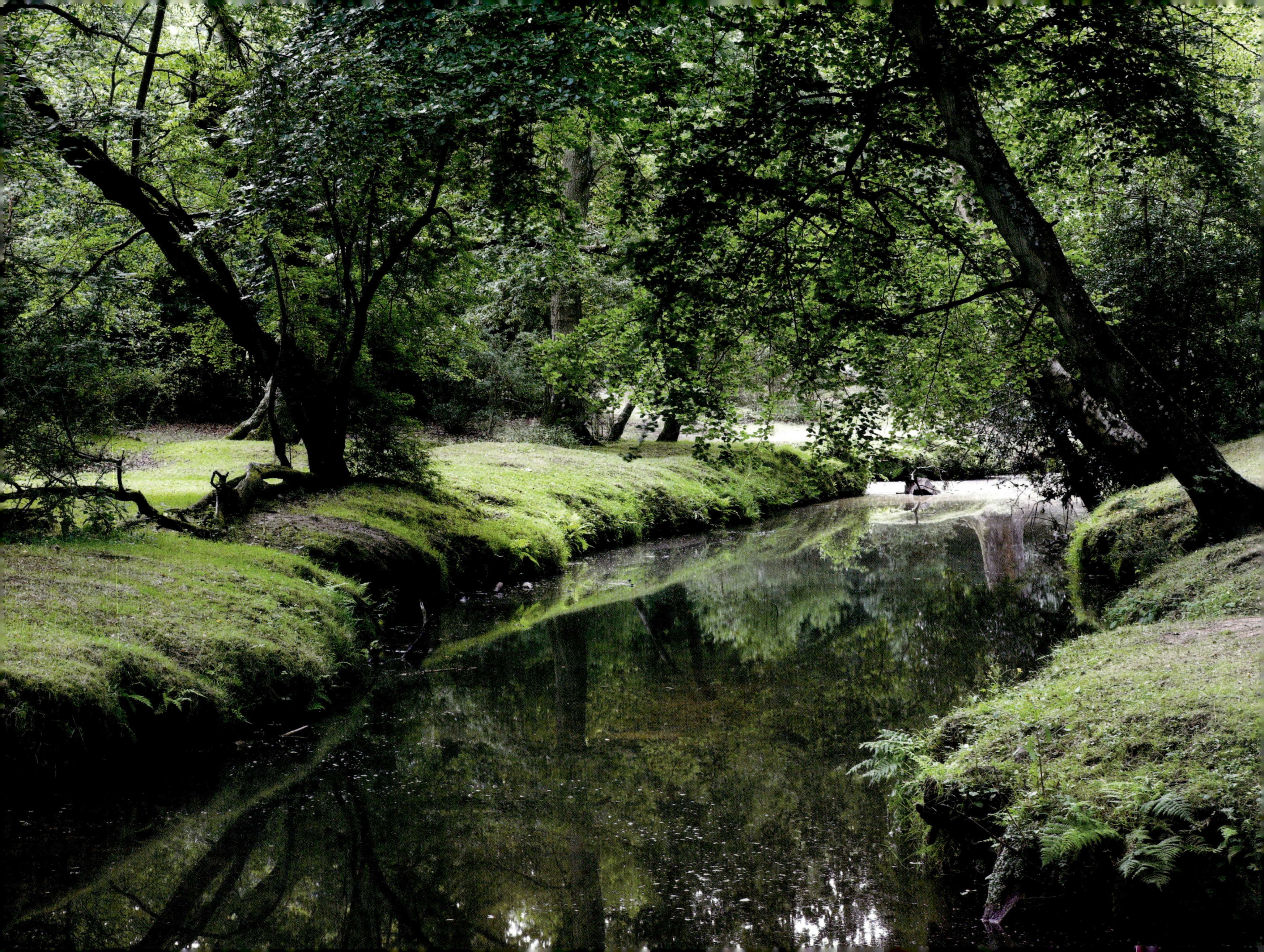

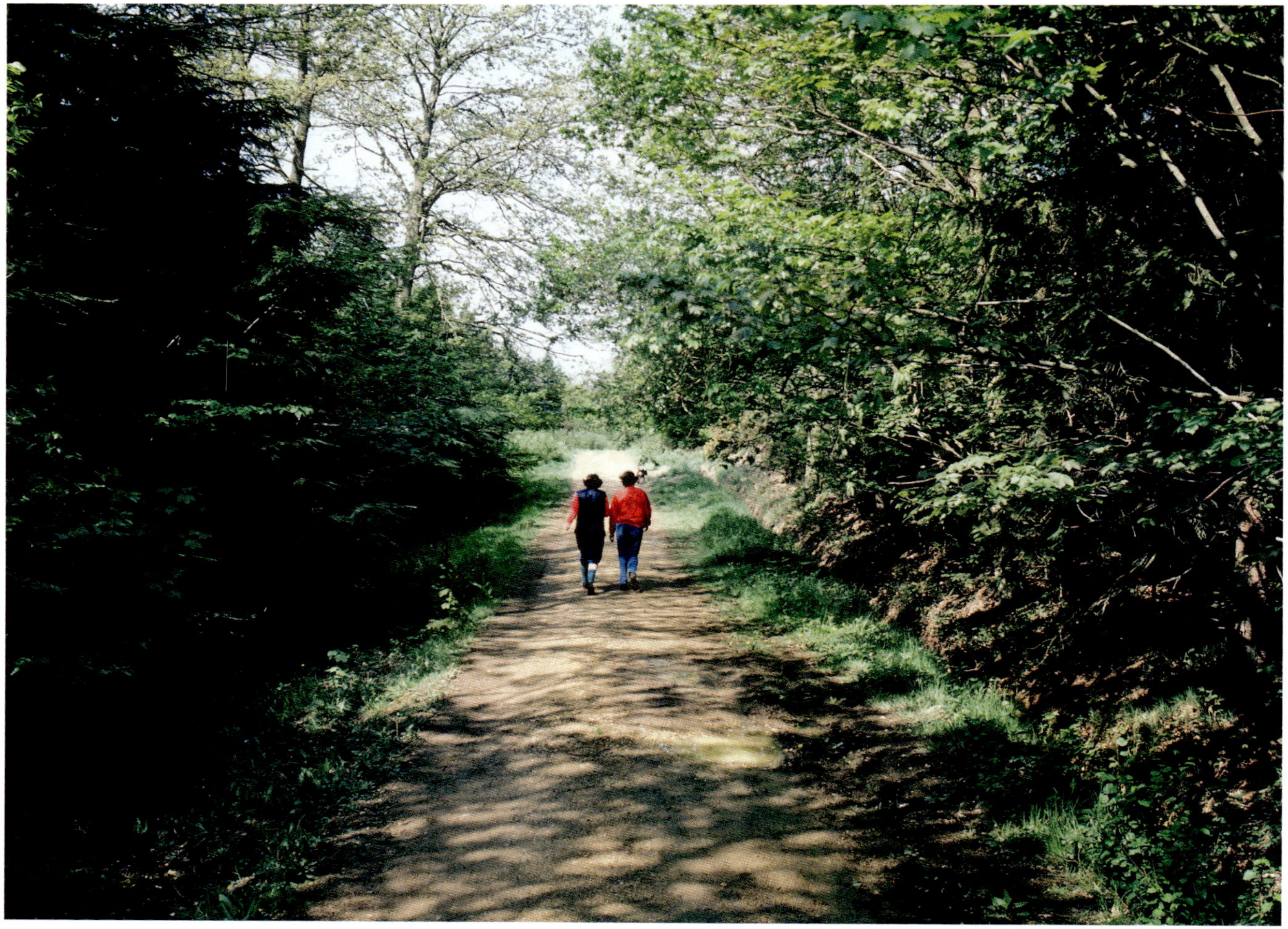

Two people walking on a track through Parkhurst Forest, Isle of Wight
Opposite: Ancient pollard oak and beech at Vinney Ridge, near Brockenhurst, New Forest

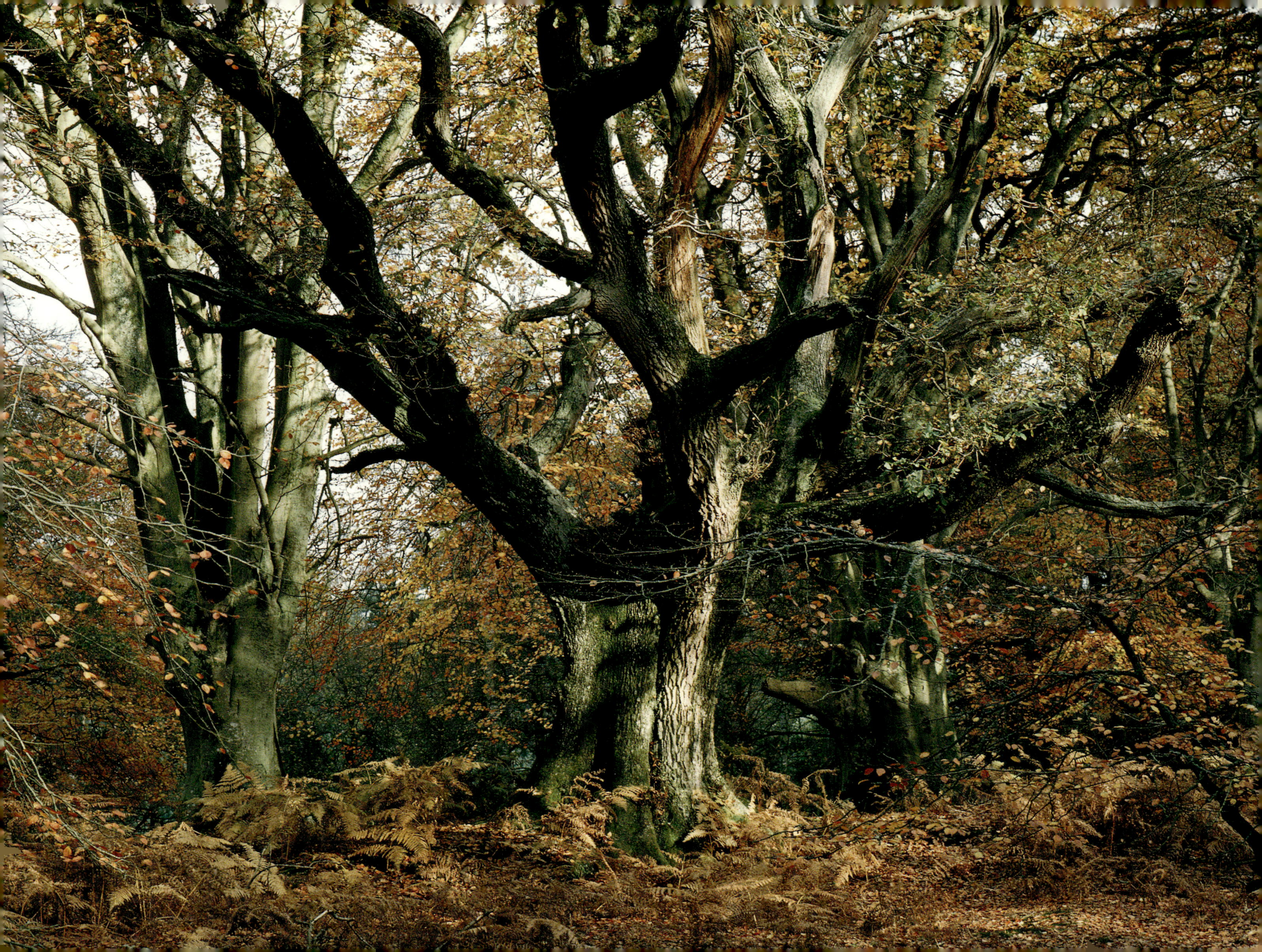

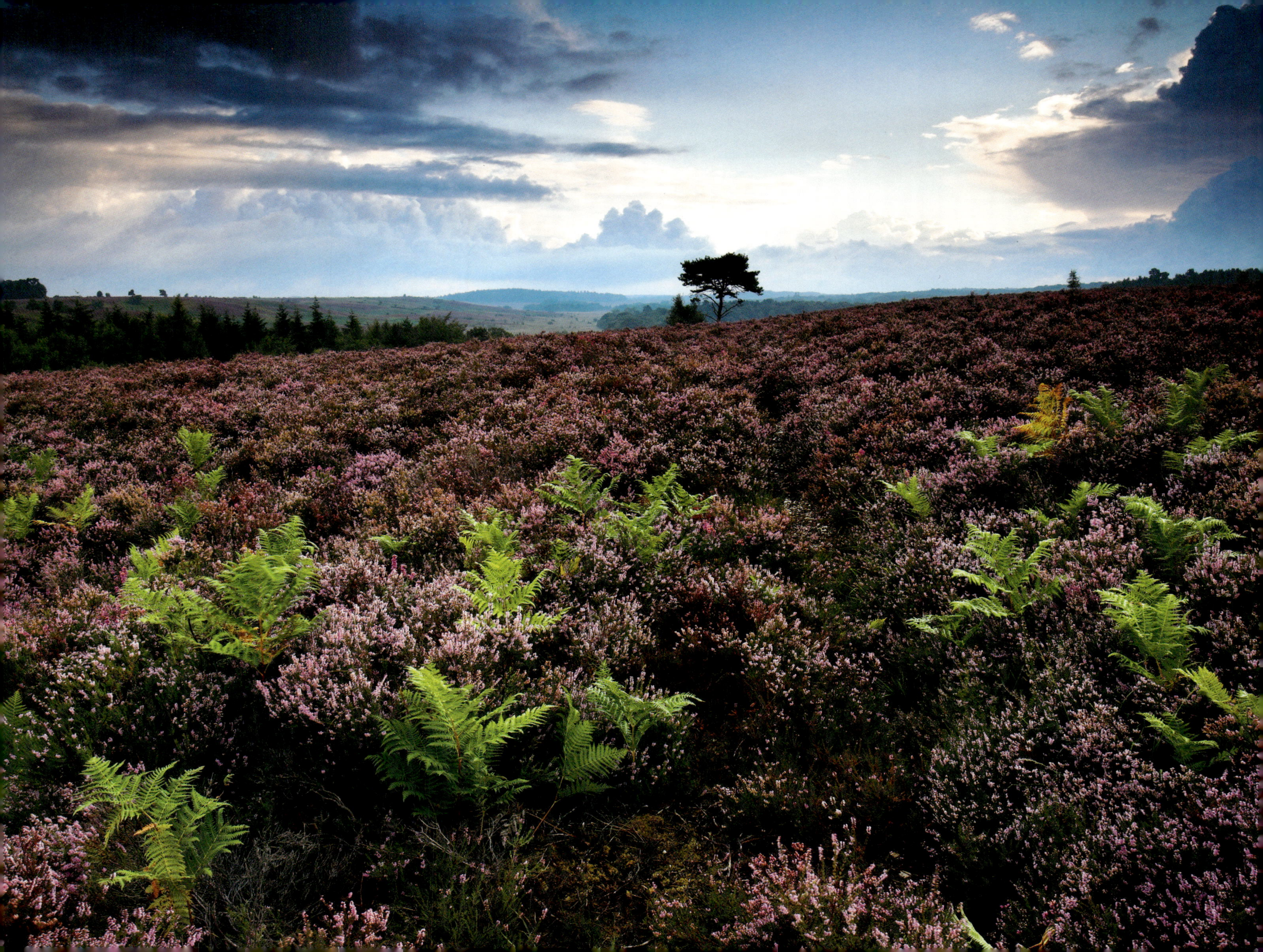

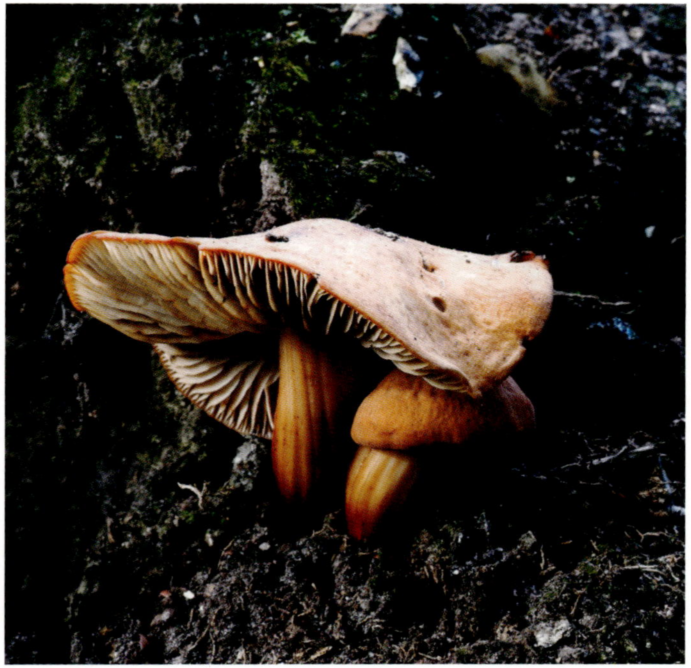

Fungi (of the agaric family) grow on the base of a fallen tree at Ipley, New Forest
Opposite: A lone Scots pine stands among a sea of pink heather at Rockford Common, New Forest

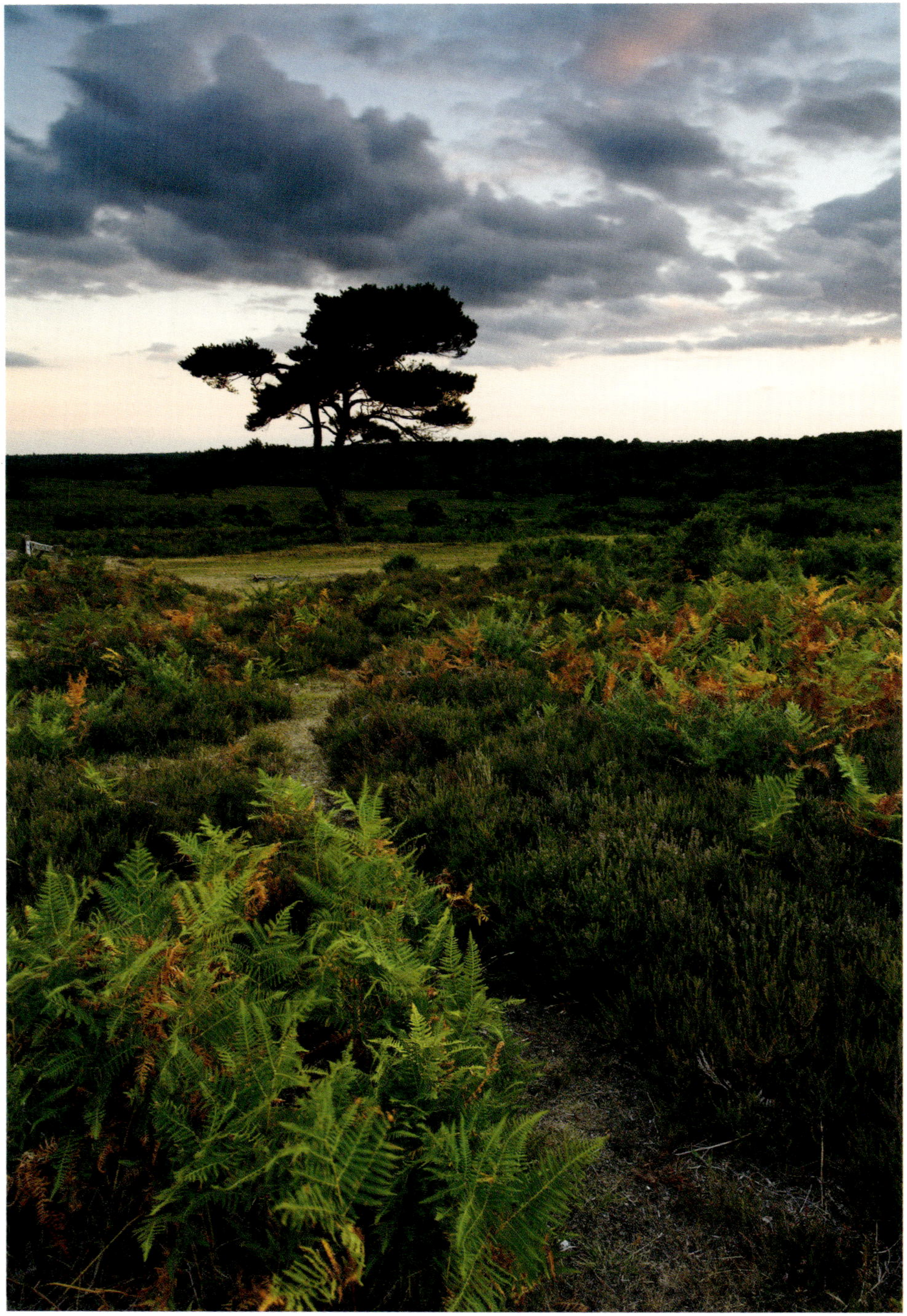

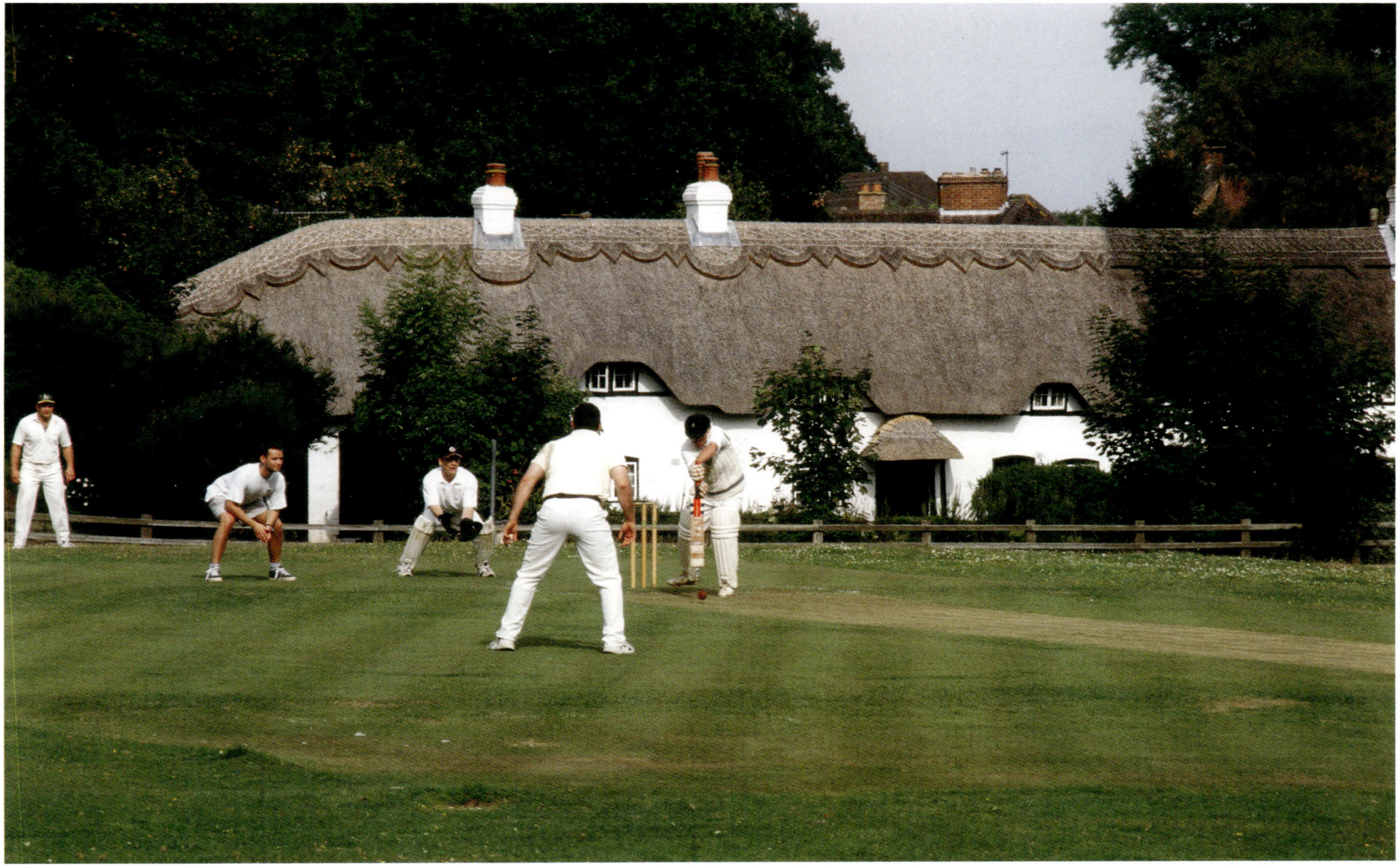

Villagers playing cricket on the green in the New Forest village of Swan Green, near Lyndhurst
Opposite: A solitary Scots pine amid heathland at Bratley View, near Picket Post in the New Forest

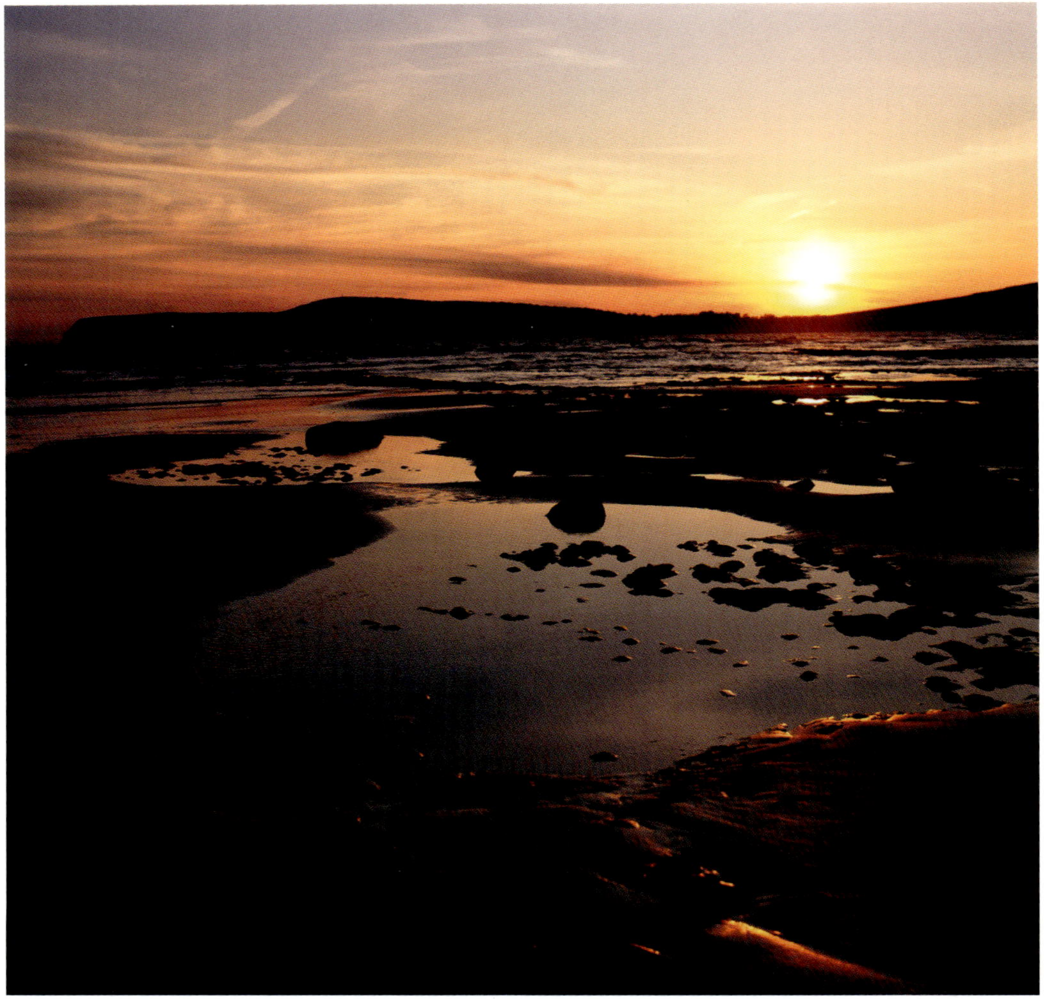

Sunset over Compton Bay, Isle of Wight
Opposite: Cottages on the 'High Street' at Buckler's Hard stretching down to the Beaulieu River

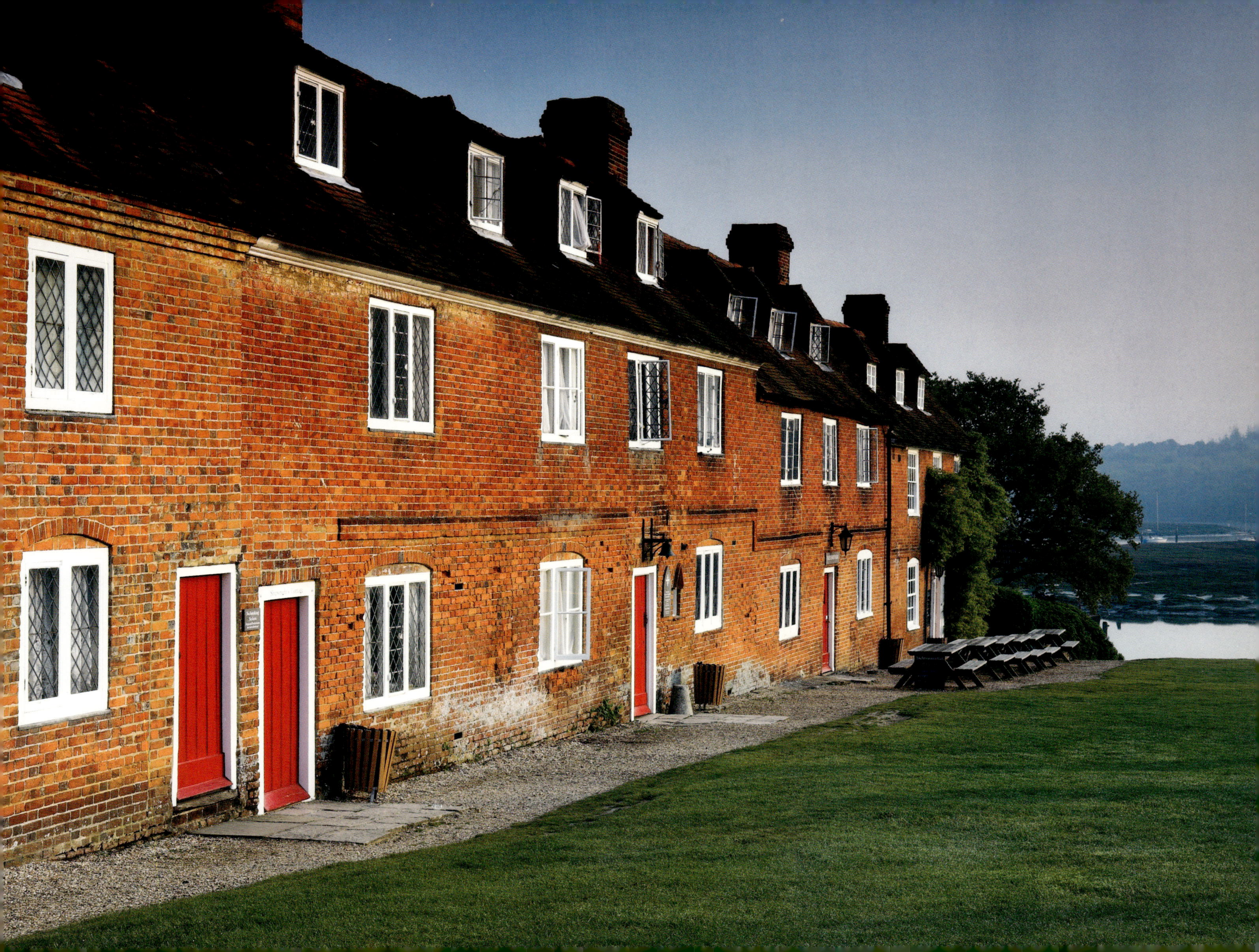

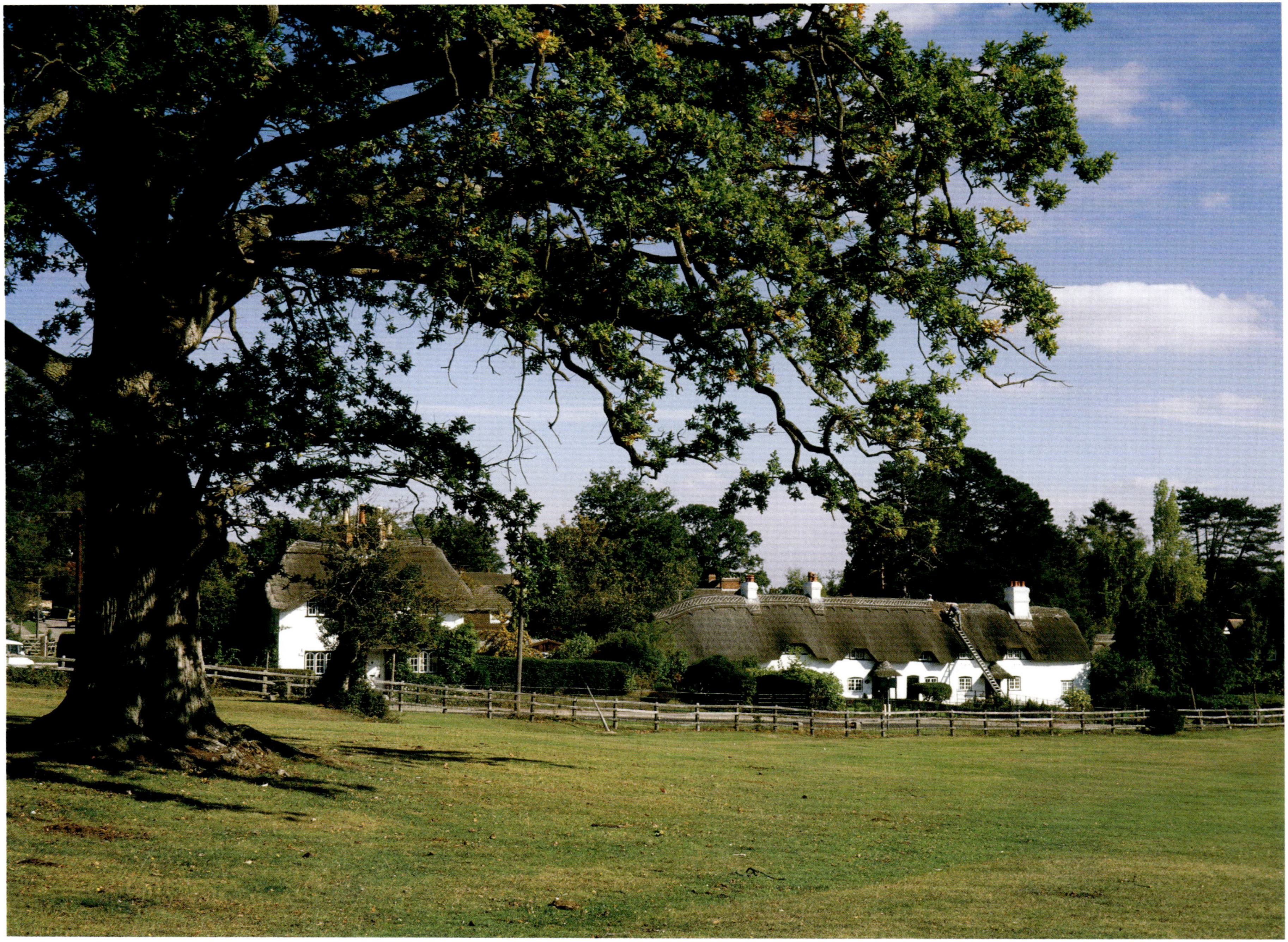

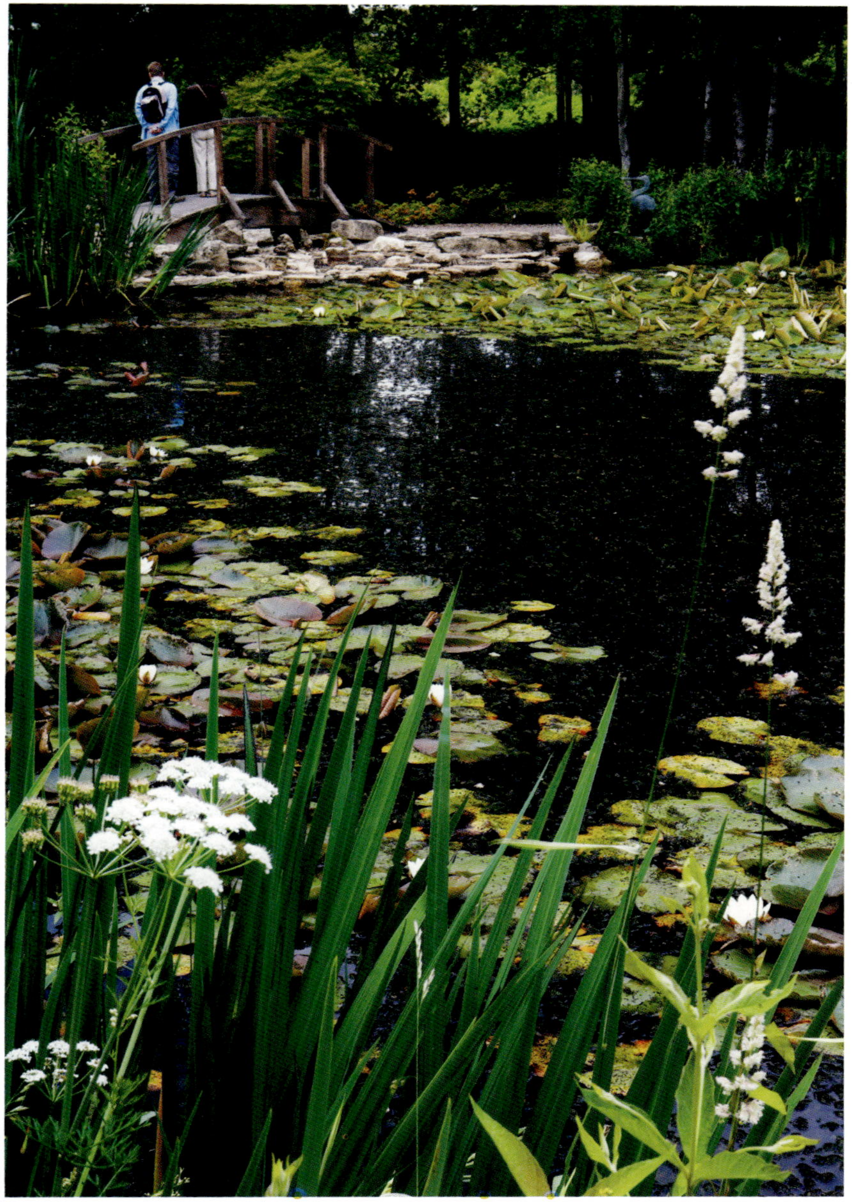

A couple standing on a small bridge over the pond at Furzey Gardens, Minstead, in the New Forest
Opposite: Swan Green hamlet overlooking thatched cottages, near Lyndhurst in the New Forest

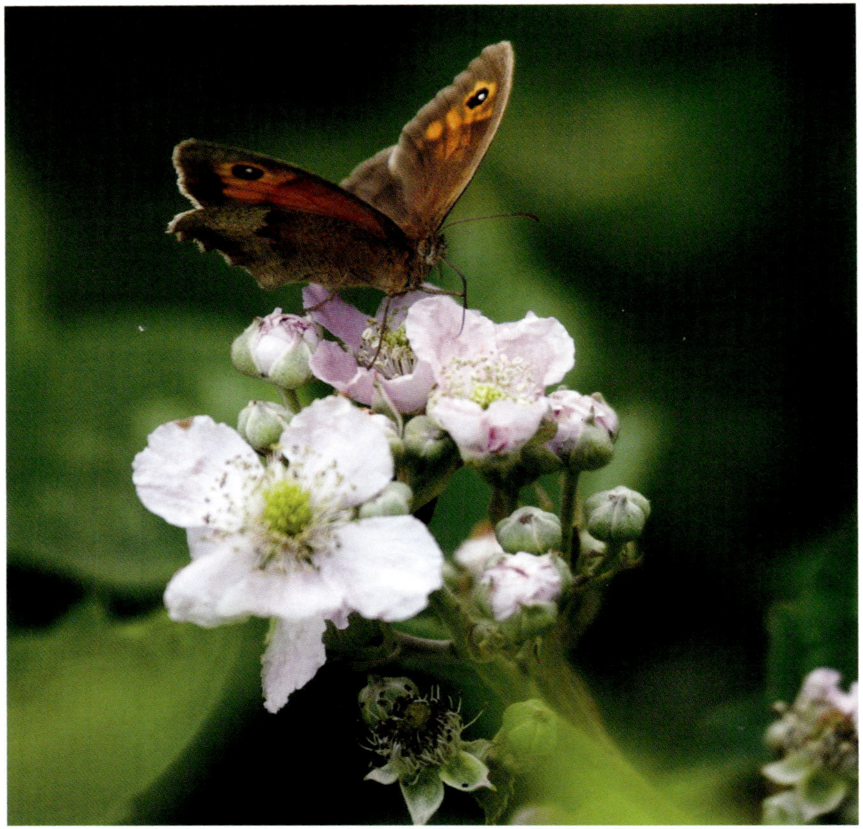

A meadow brown butterfly in the Adgestone Vineyard, Isle of Wight

Opposite: The remains of a pier used for the D-Day embarkation at Lepe, near Calshot at the mouth of Southampton Water

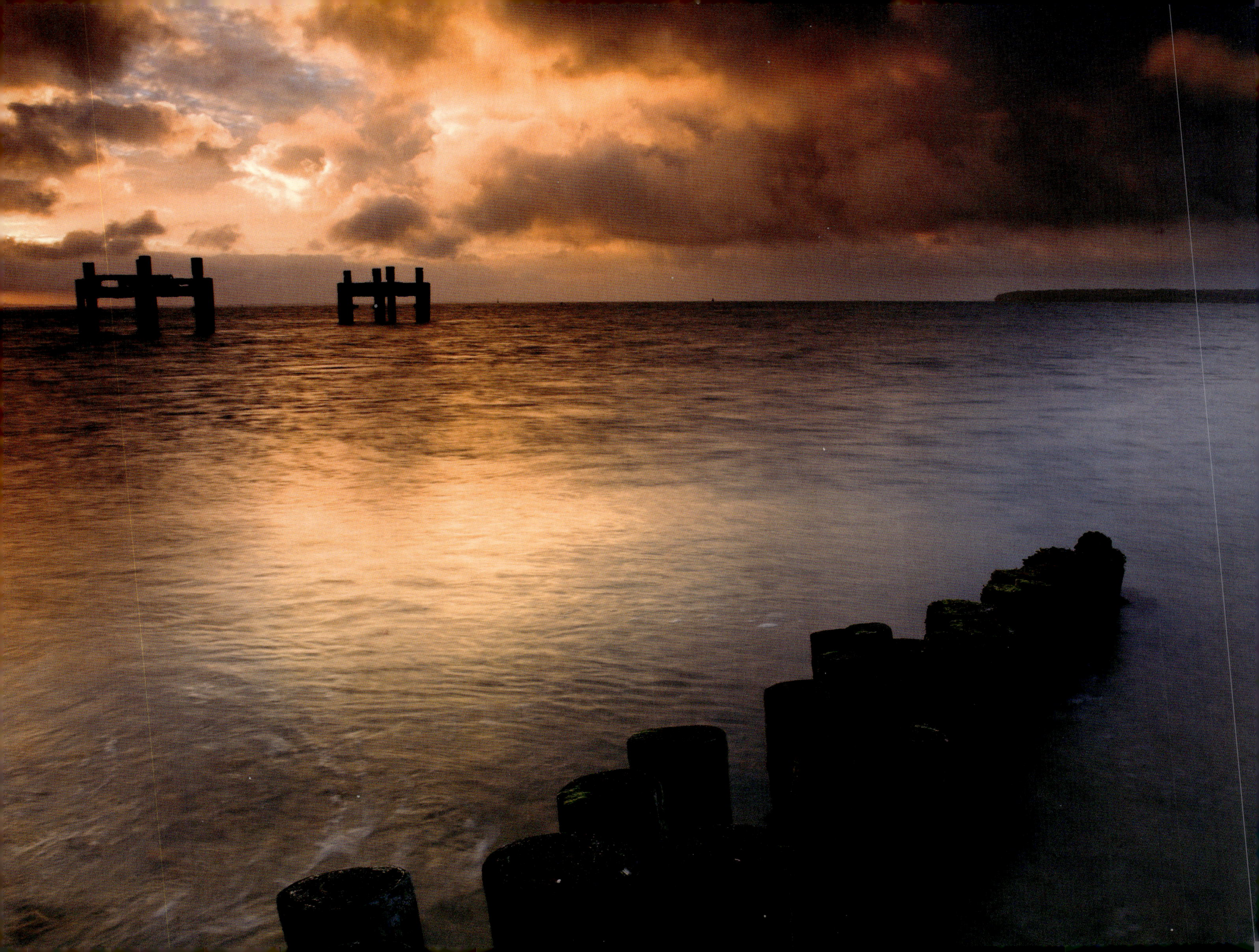

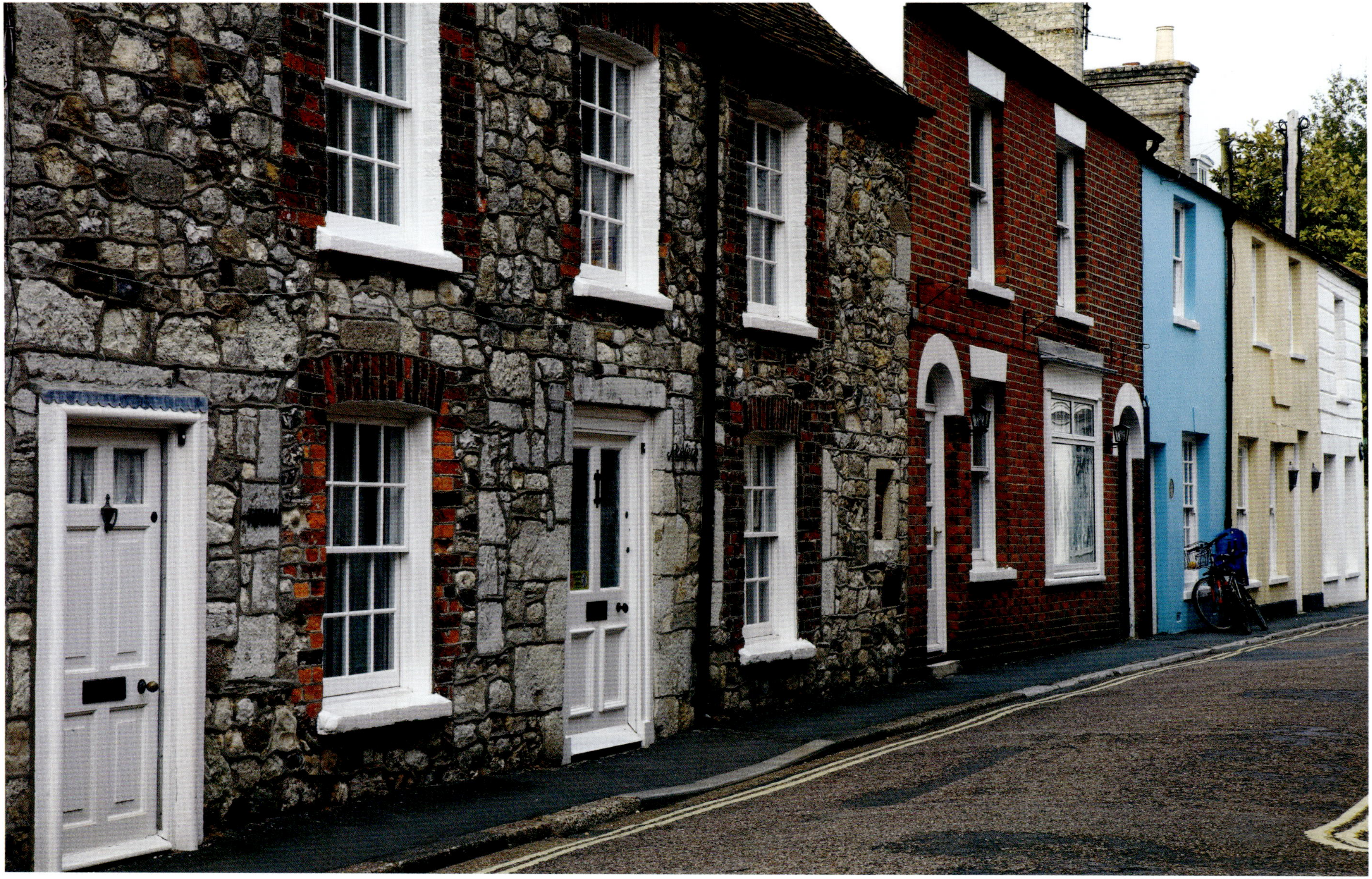

Terrace houses line a Yarmouth street in the Isle of Wight

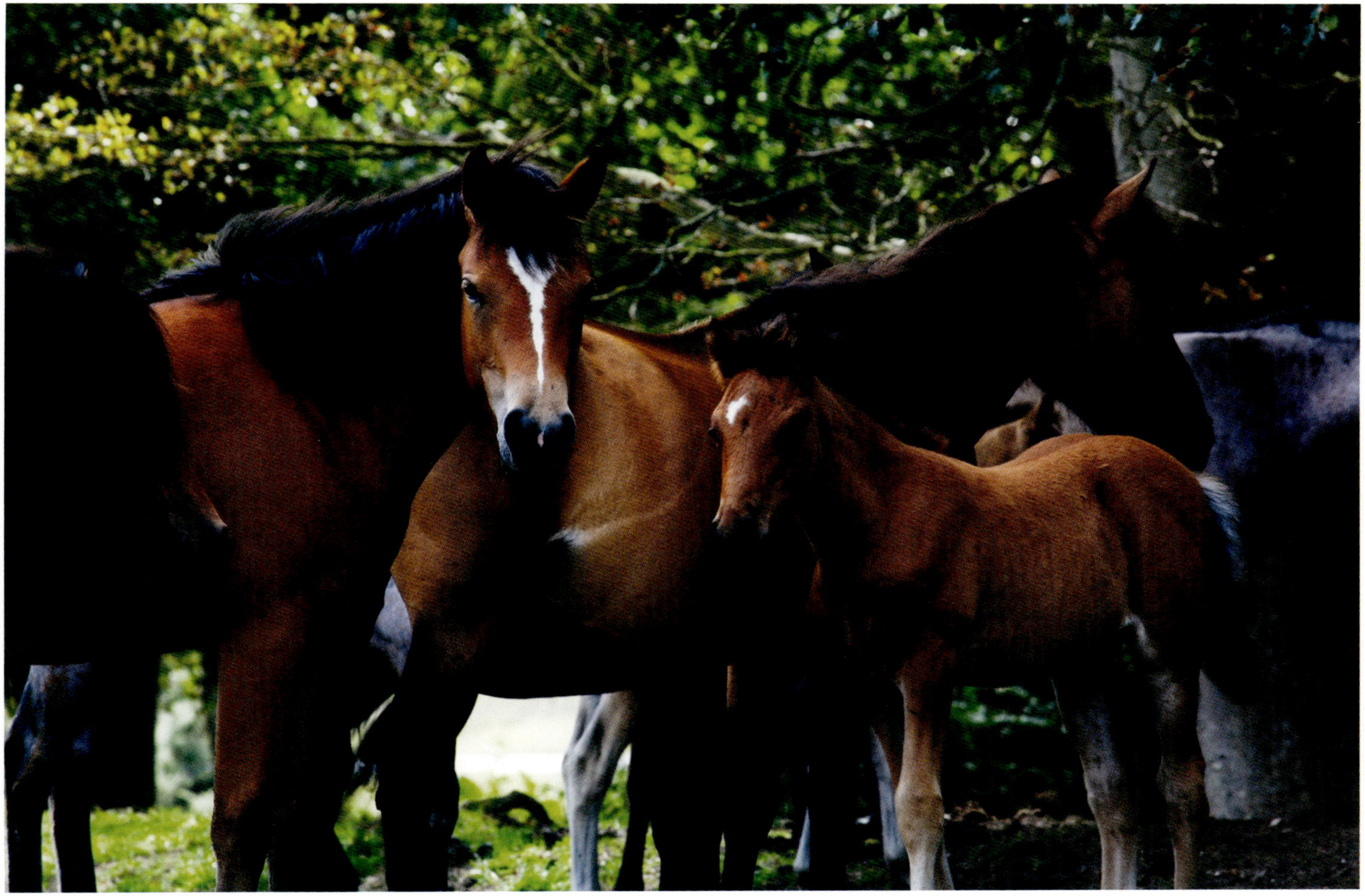

New Forest ponies congregate under the trees to escape the summer sun

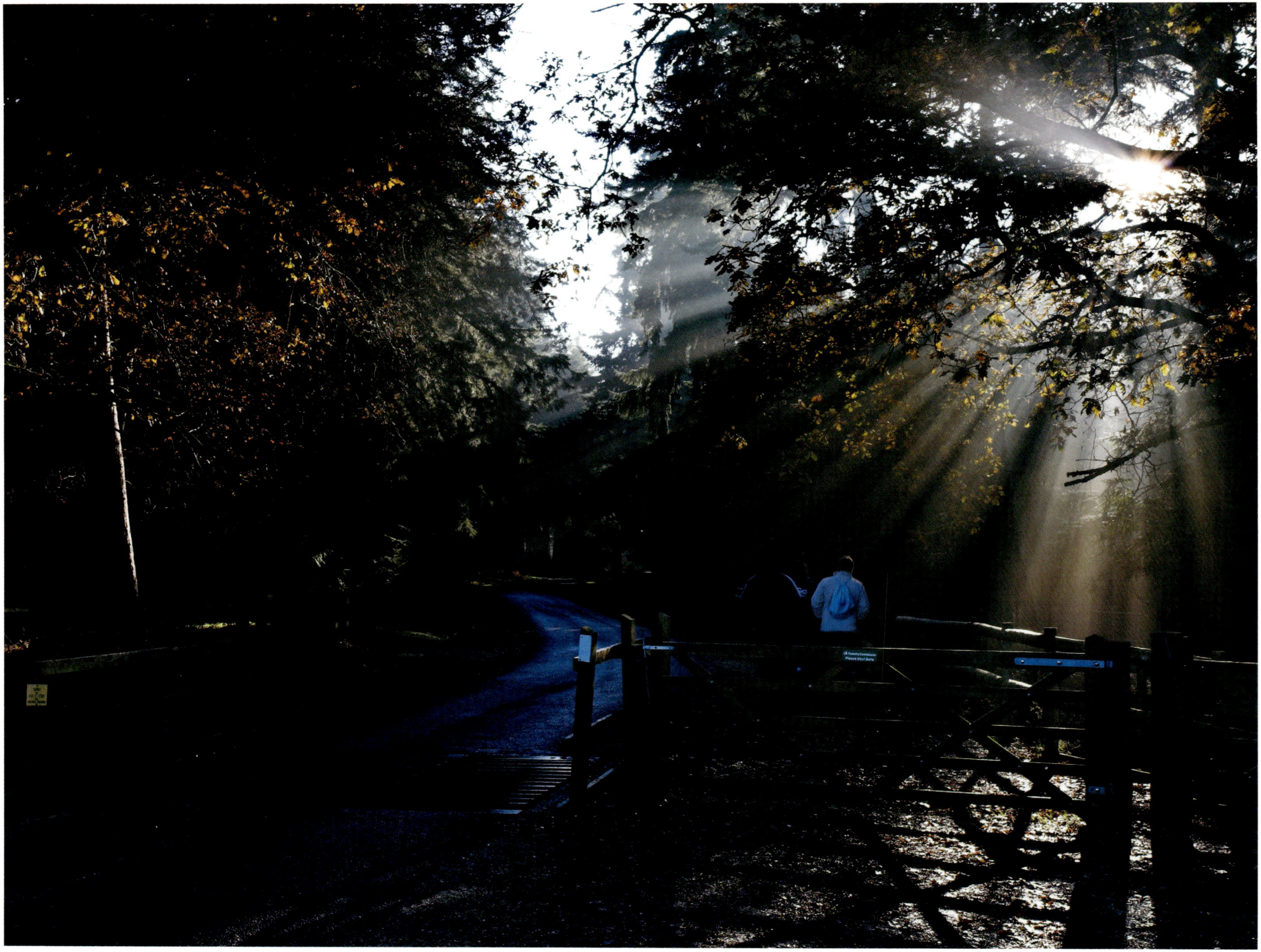

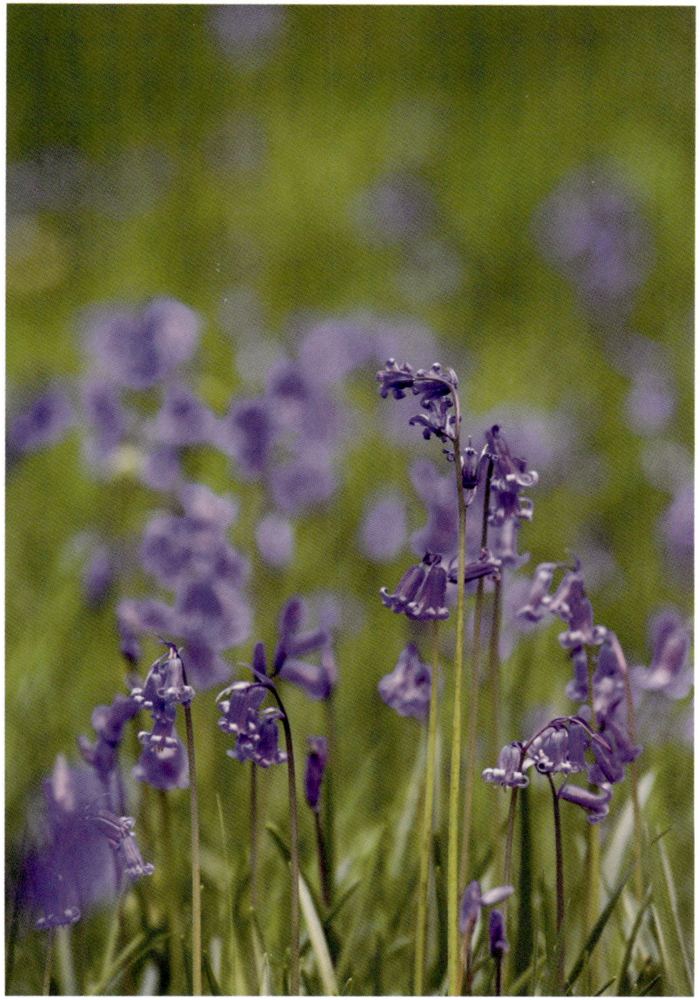

Bluebells by a roadside in Beaulieu

Opposite: A burst of sunlight shines upon walkers at the Ornamental Drive at Bolderwood, New Forest

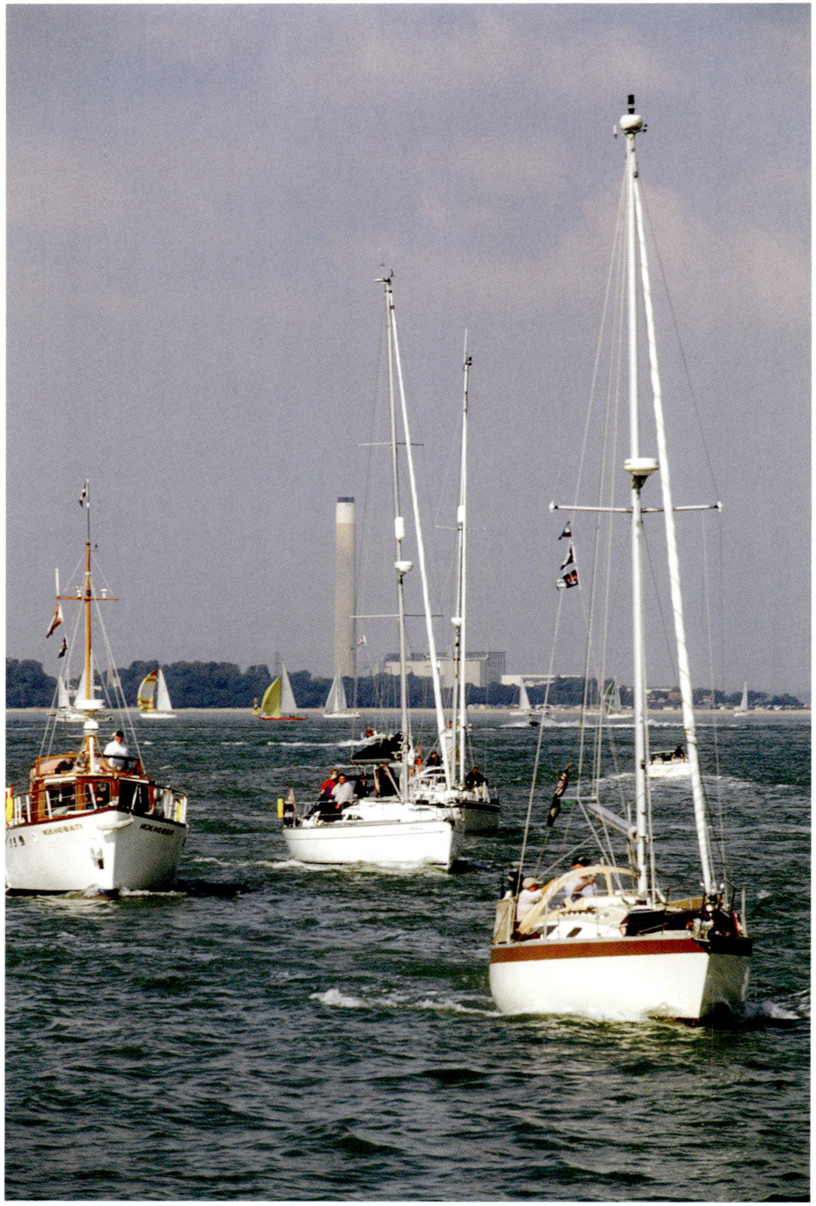

Sailing boats in the Solent with Calshot and its power station in the background

Opposite: A whitewashed building on the clifftop in the heart of Freshwater Bay, known as the 'Tennyson Heritage Coast' on the Isle of Wight

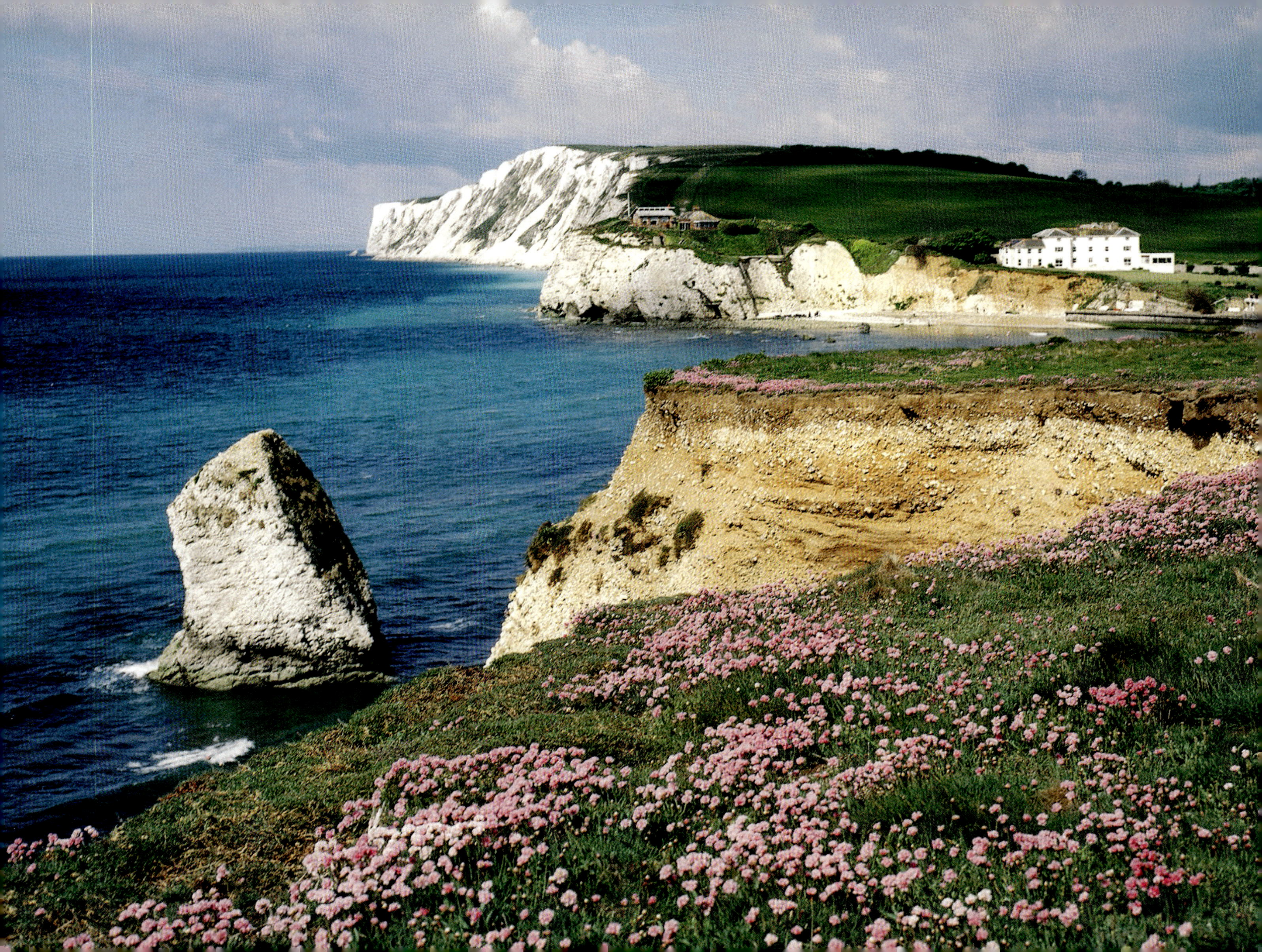

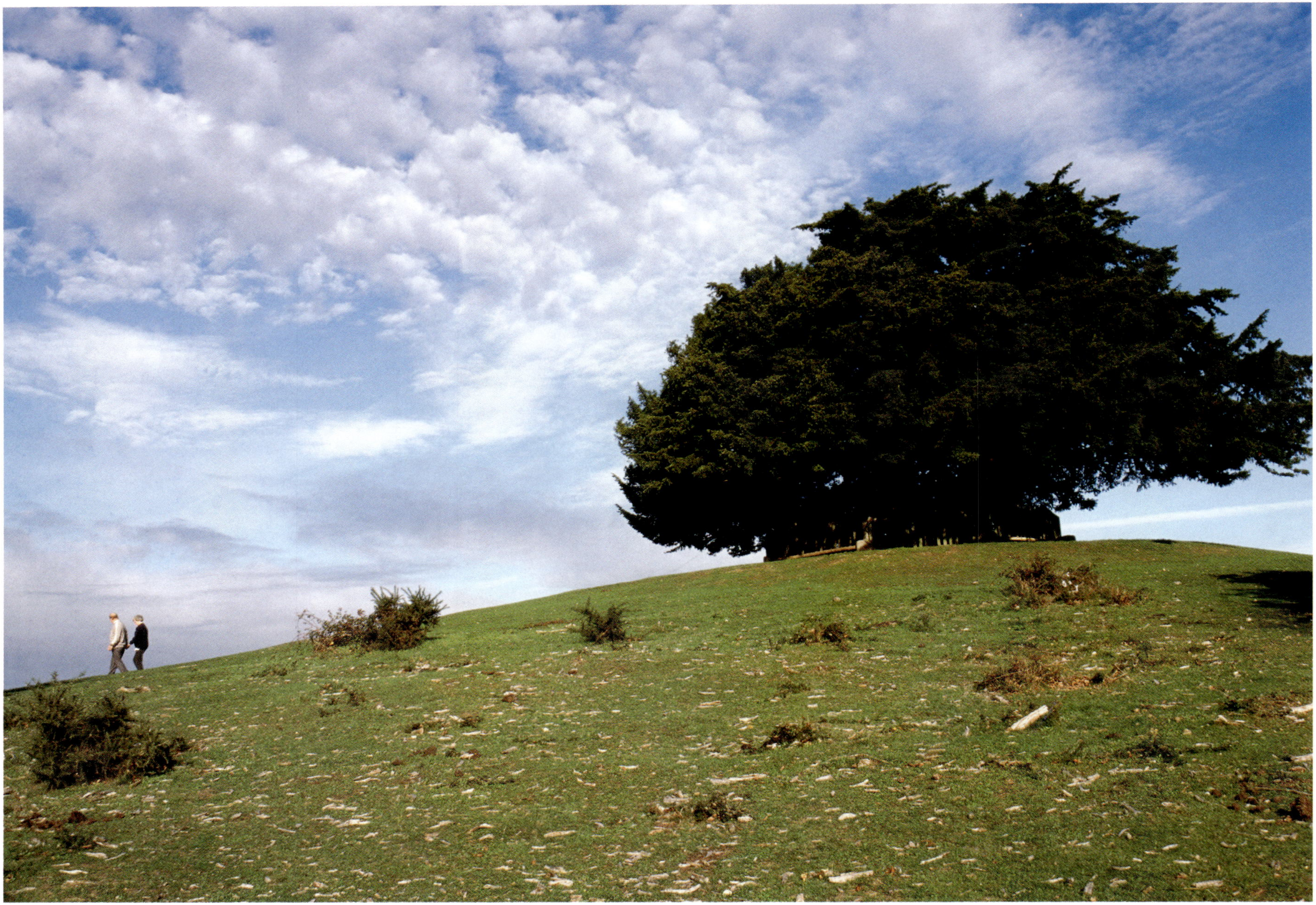

A giant yew stands on the brow of a hill at Bolton's Bench, Lyndhurst, named after the Duke of Bolton, 18th-century Keeper of the Forest

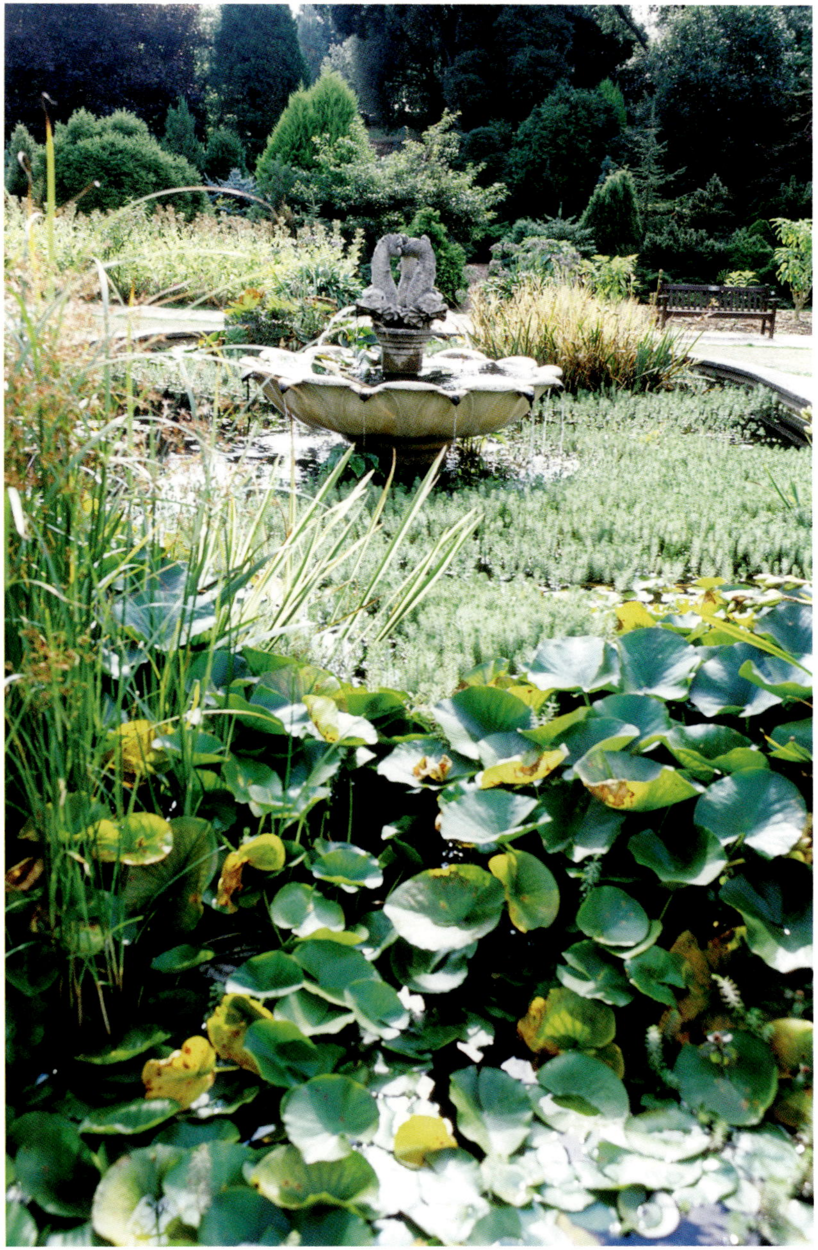

Fountain in the Botanic Gardens at Ventnor on the Isle of Wight

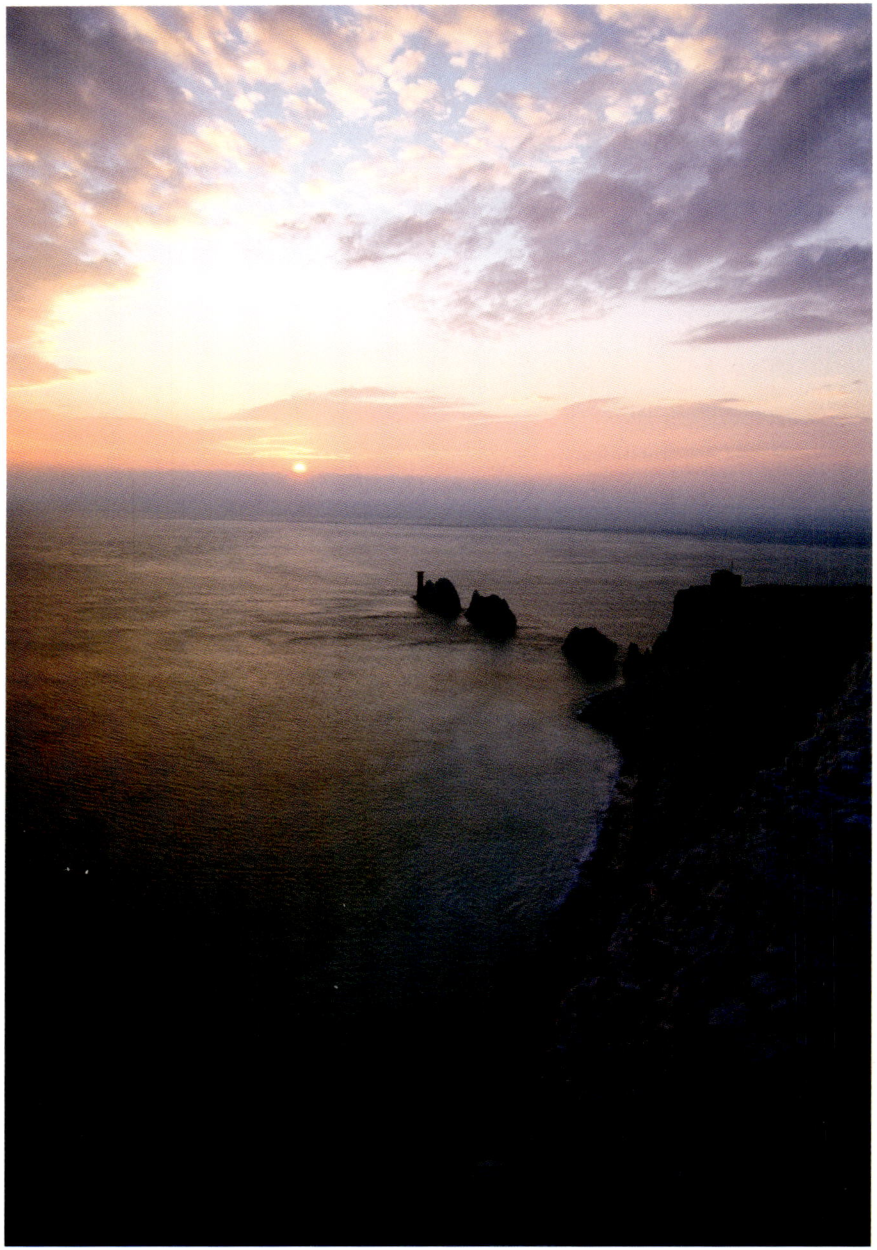

The Needles on the Isle of Wight at dusk

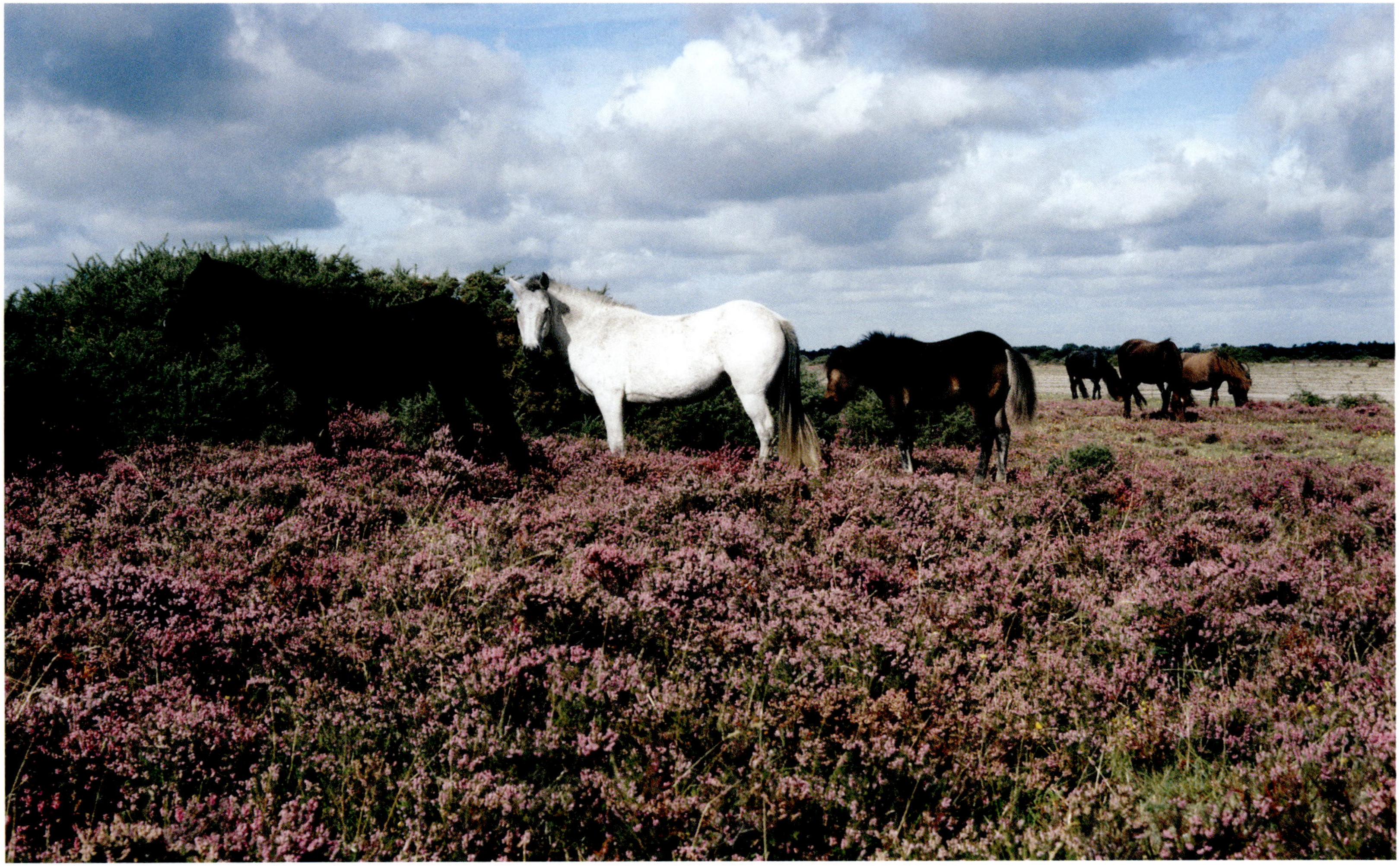

New Forest ponies on a carpet of heather

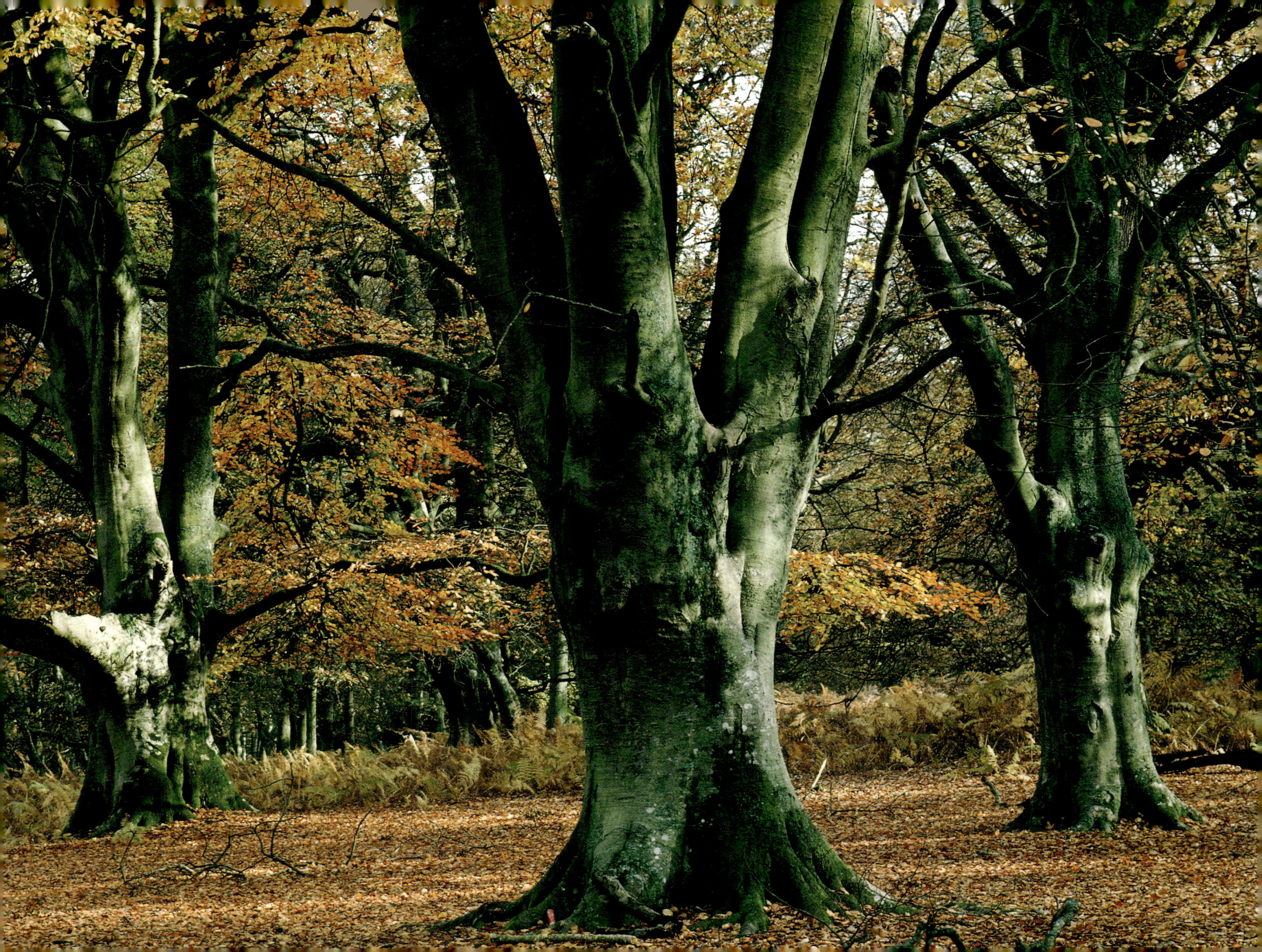

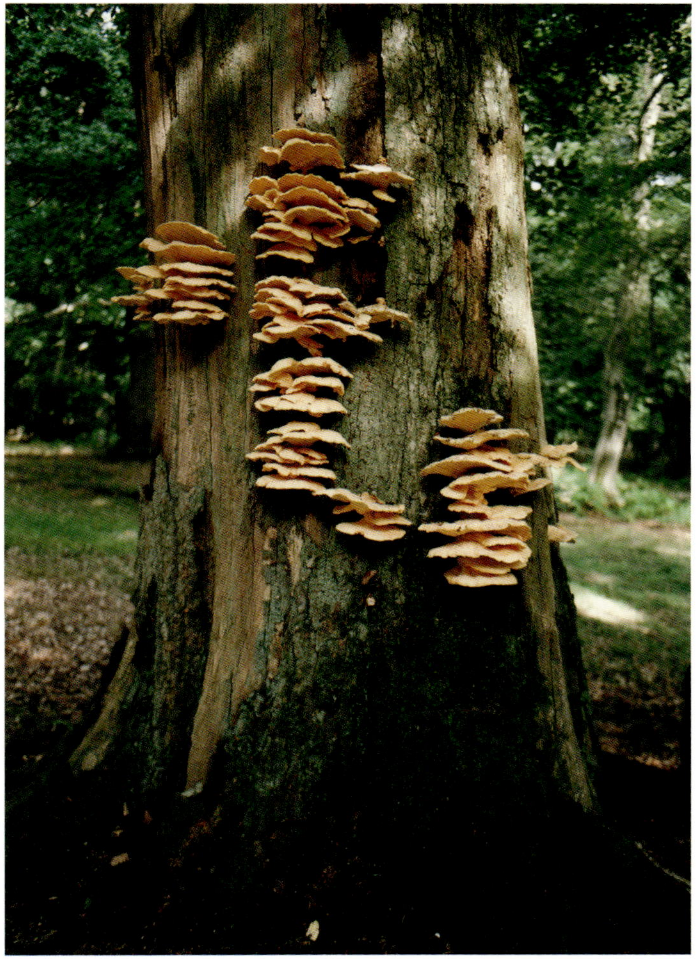

Bracket fungi on a tree trunk in the New Forest
Opposite: Autumnal leaf litter surrounds pollarded beeches on Vinney Ridge in the New Forest

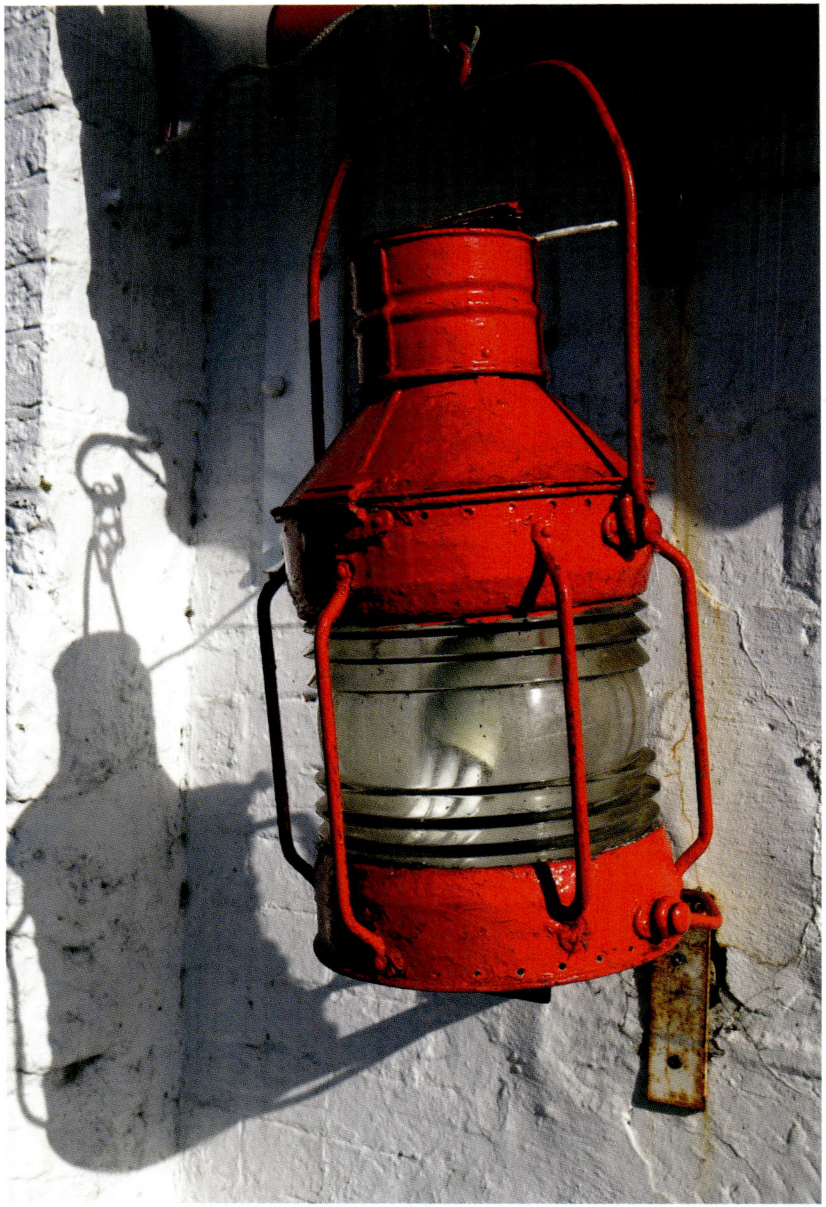

An old red 'hurricane' lamp outside a shop in Bembridge, Isle of Wight
Opposite: Sunrise over the Bembridge houseboat 'Day Dawn'

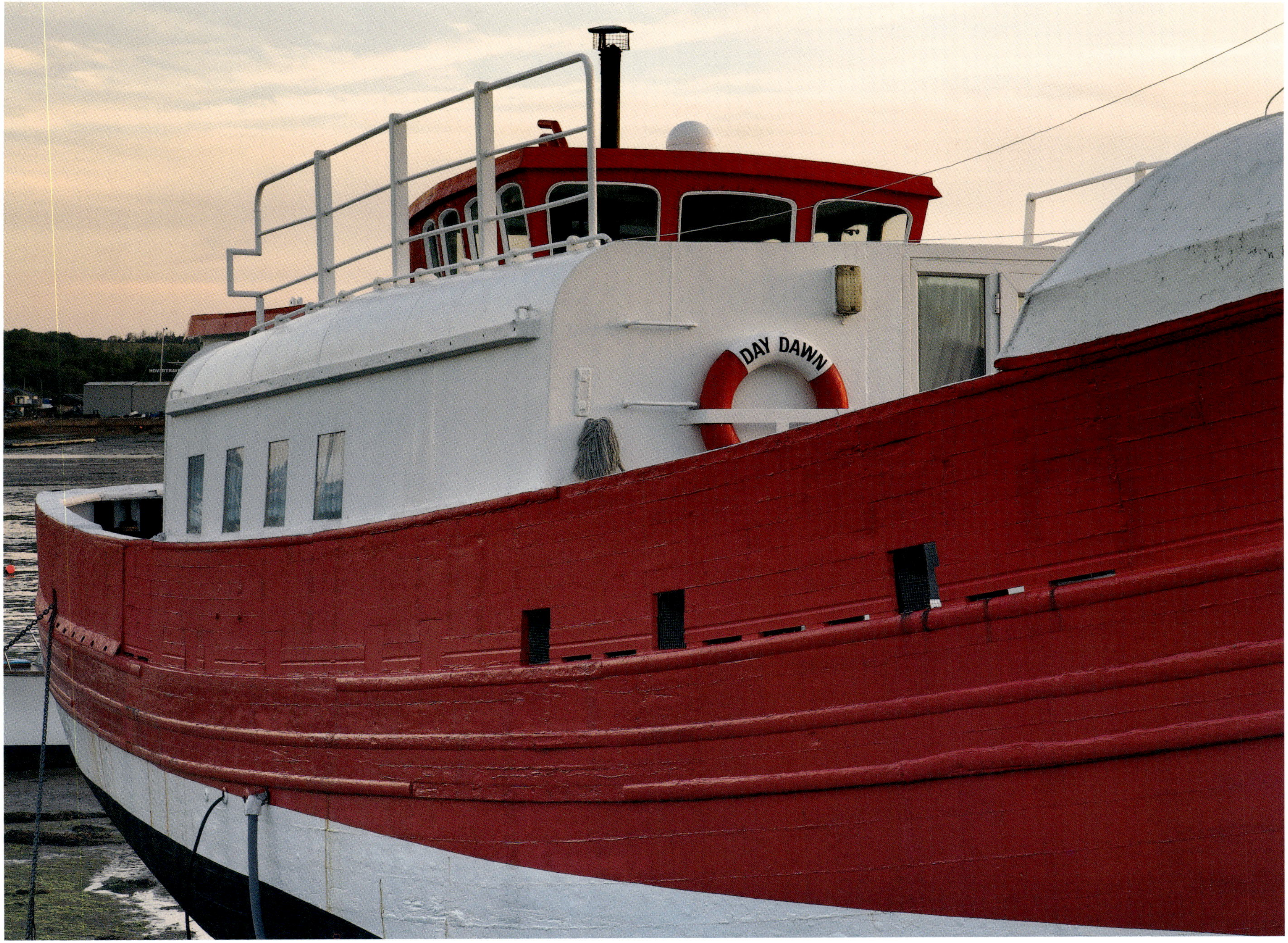
DAY DAWN

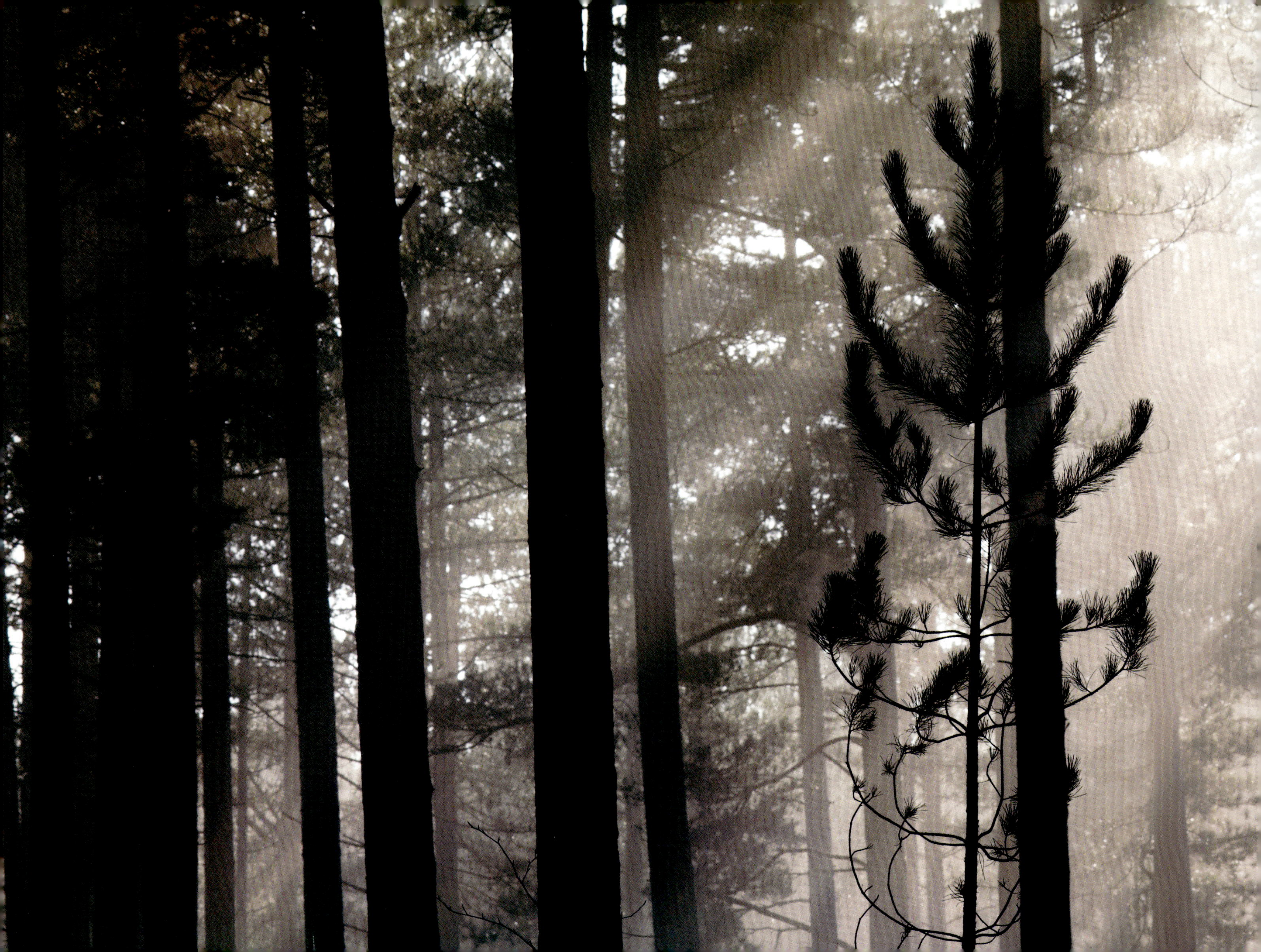

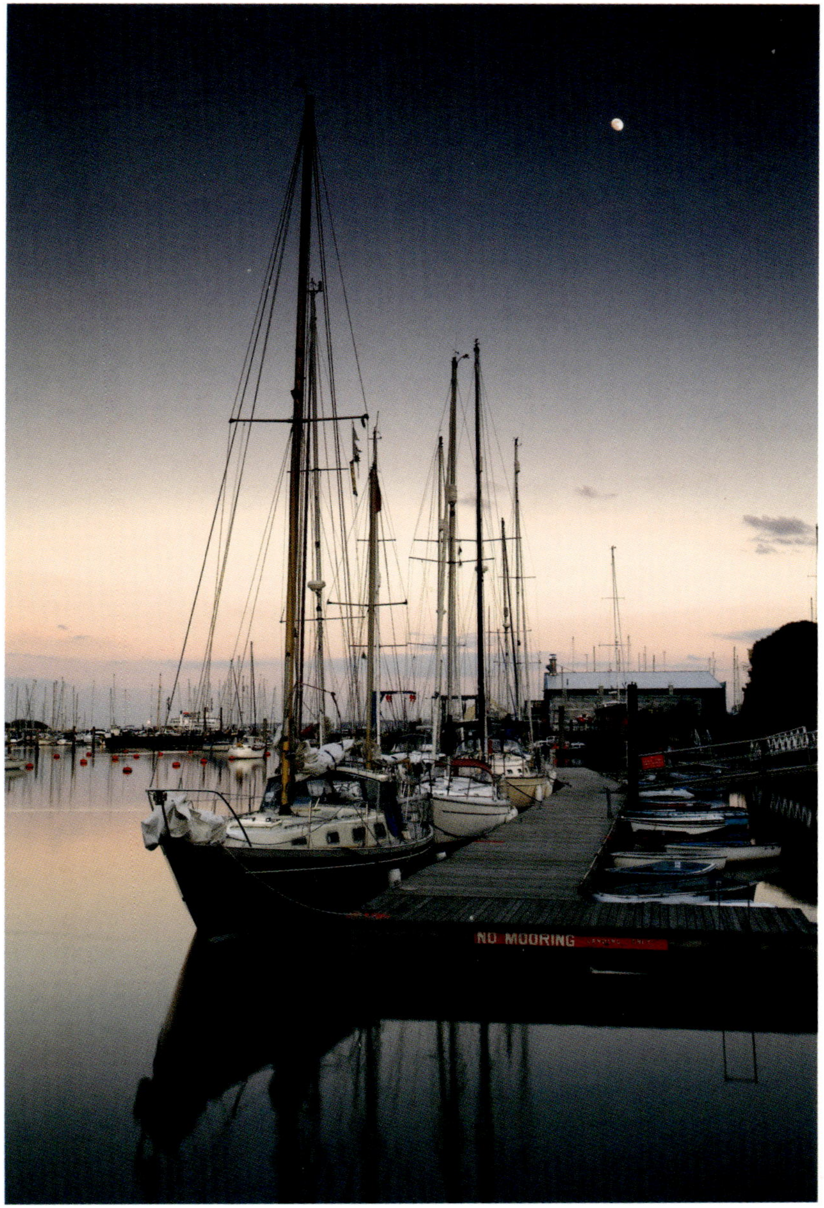

Moonlight over a peaceful evening at Lymington harbour

Opposite: A young tree grows in a Scots pine plantation near Burley, New Forest

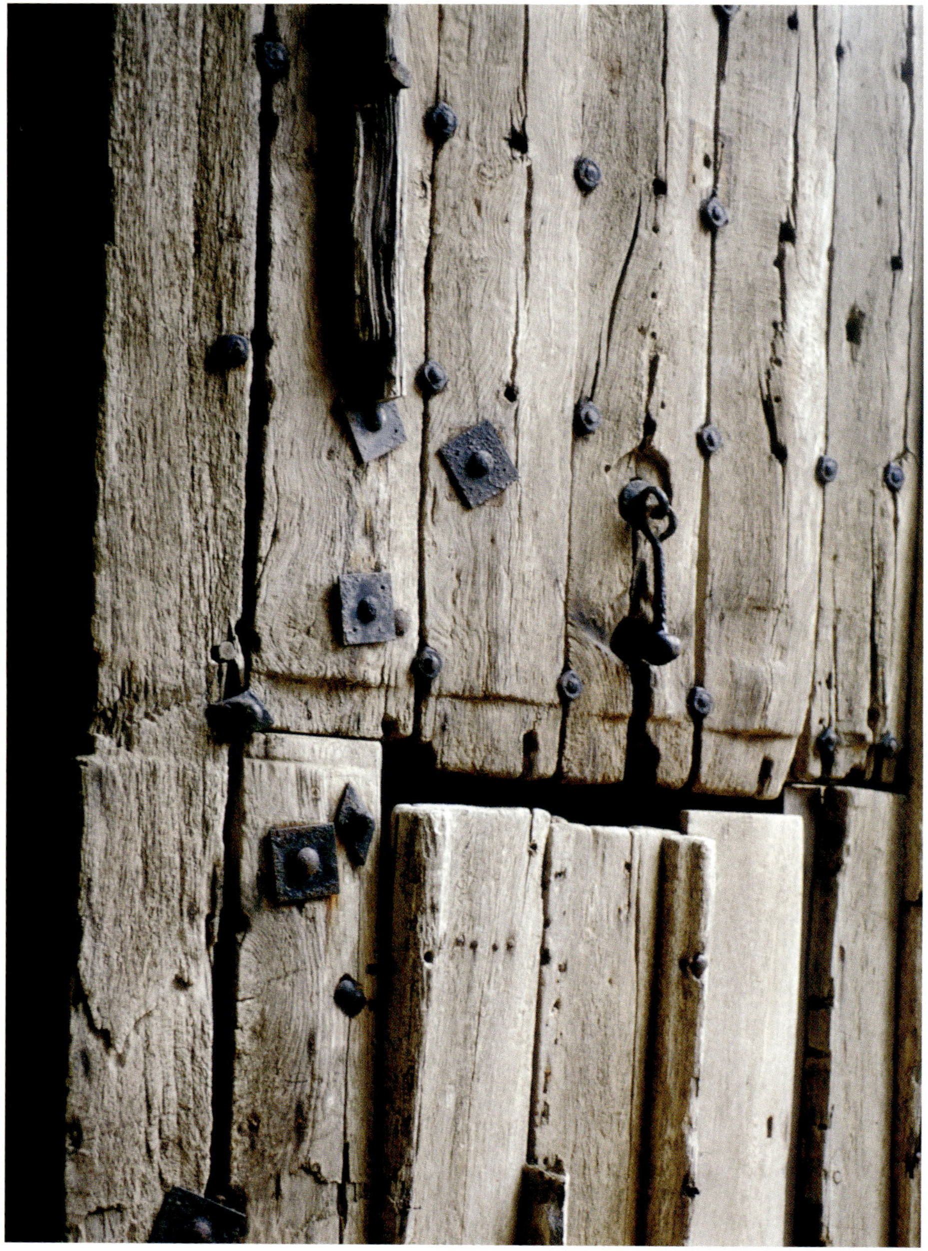

Detail of the medieval doors of Carisbrooke Castle – the Isle of Wight's royal castle which was also famous as a prison to Charles I

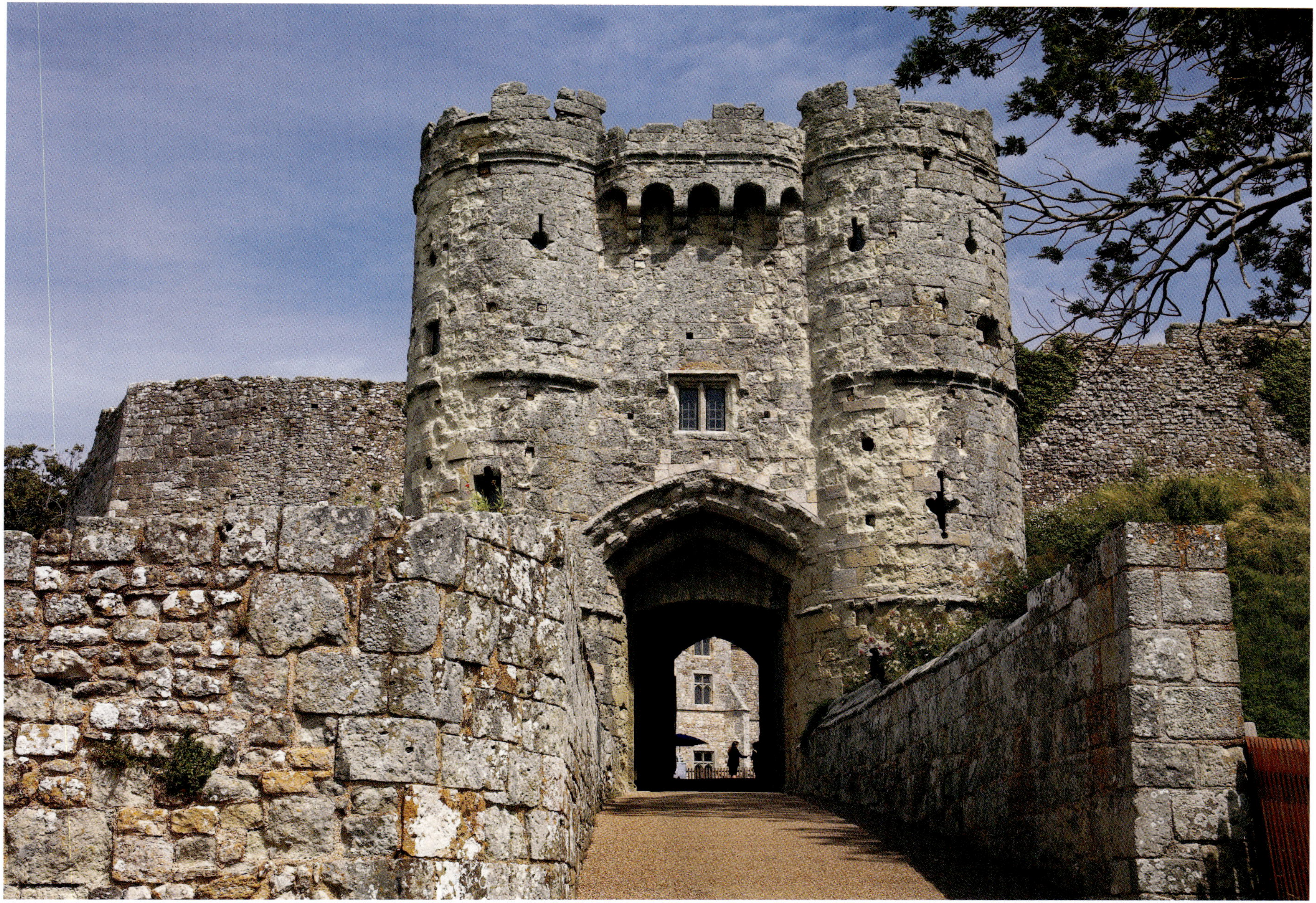

The imposing twin-towered gatehouse of Carisbrooke Castle

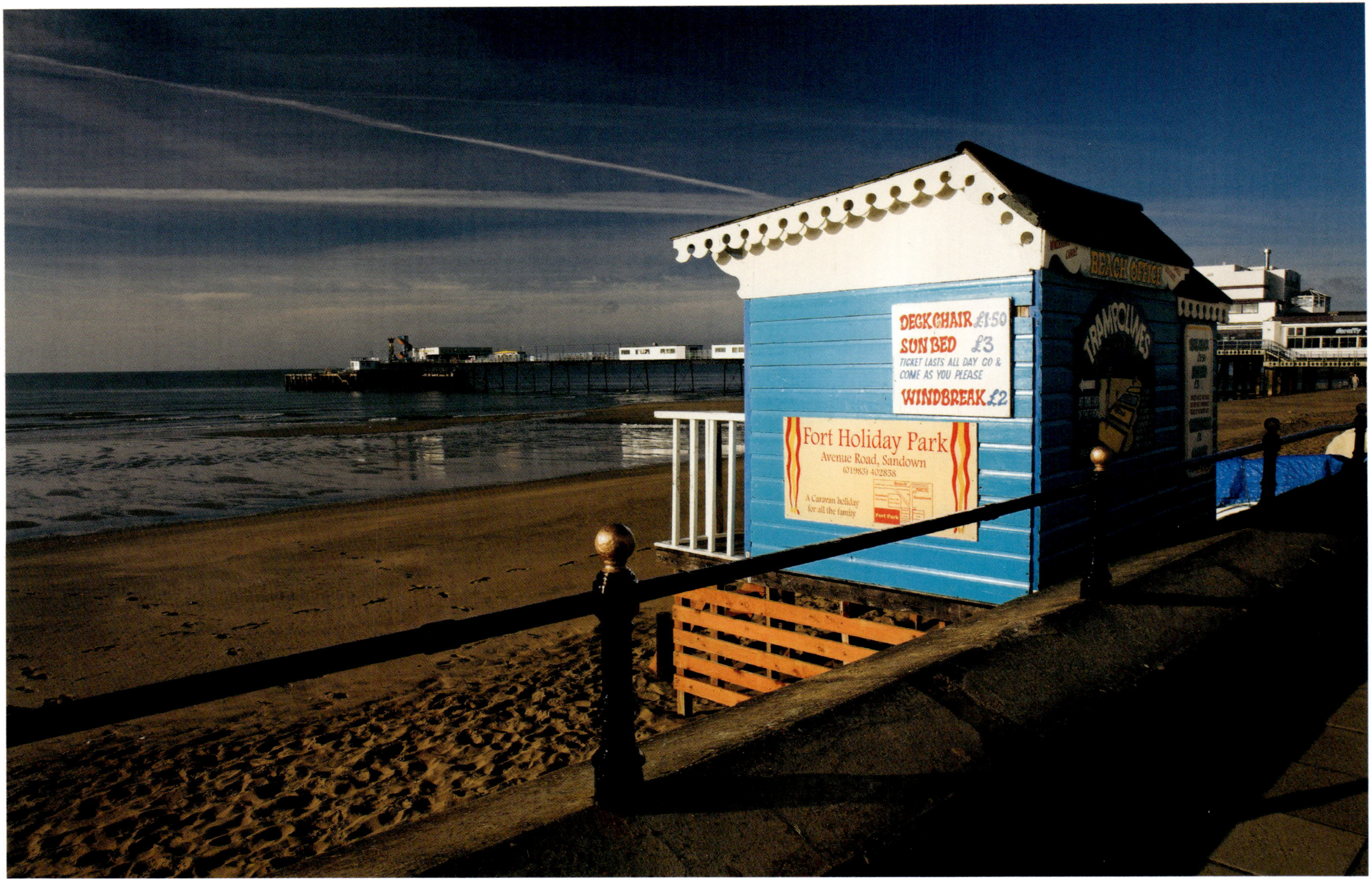

The pier and beach office at Sandown, Isle of Wight

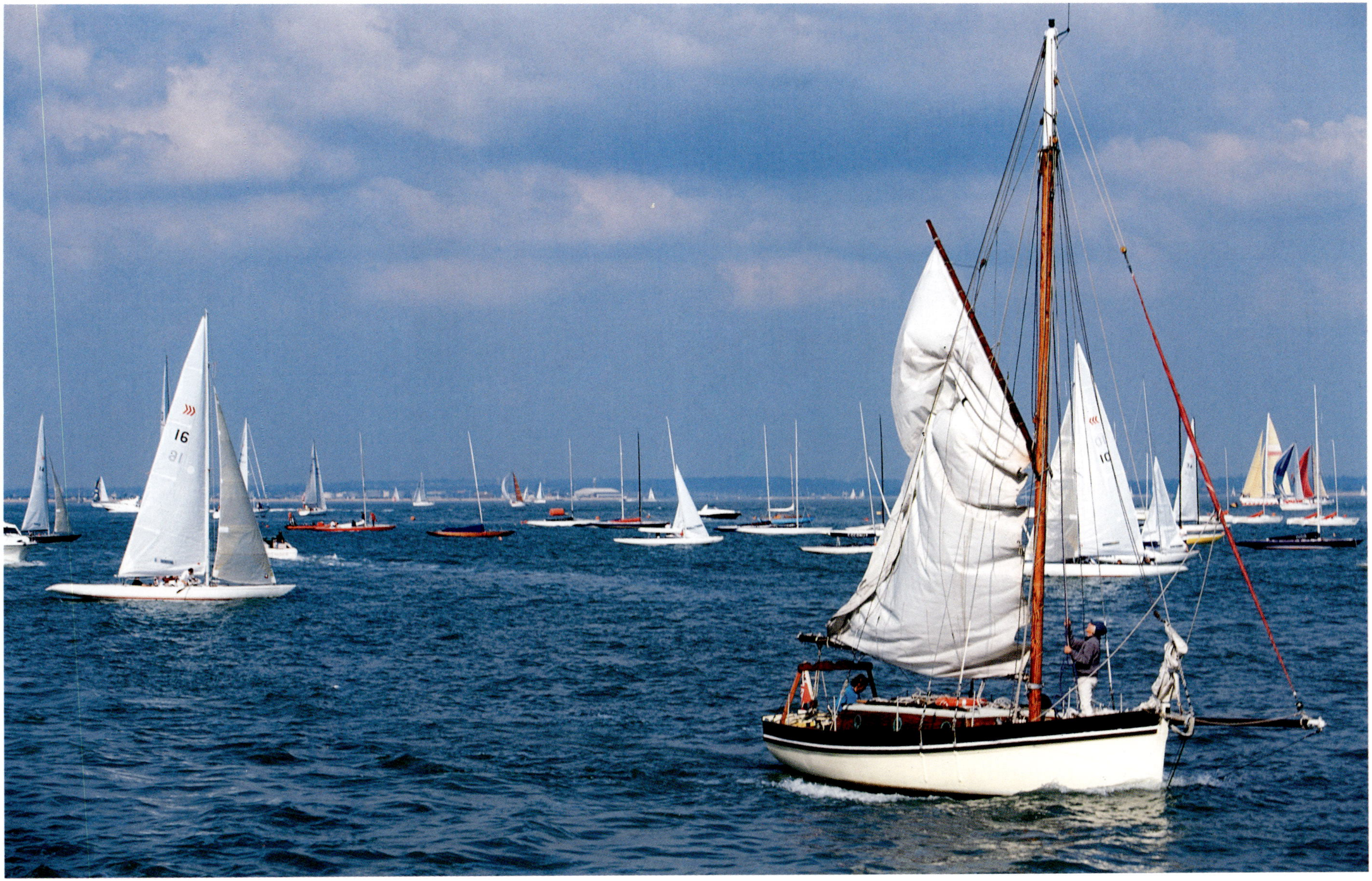

Sailing boats in Cowes harbour entrance, Isle of Wight

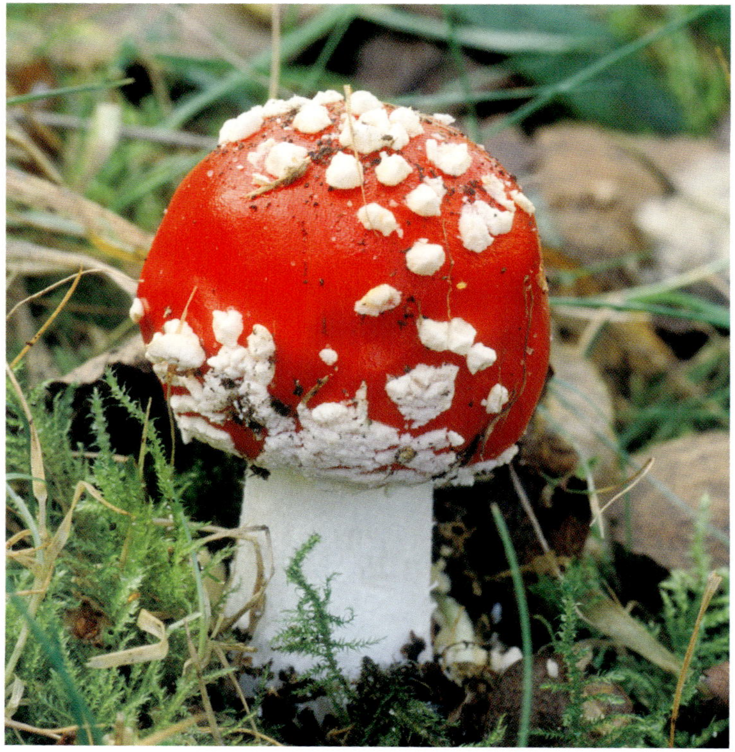

A red-and-white spotted 'fly agaric' fungus photographed in the New Forest
Opposite: A groyne zig-zags down the beach, pointing to the Isle of Wight on the horizon

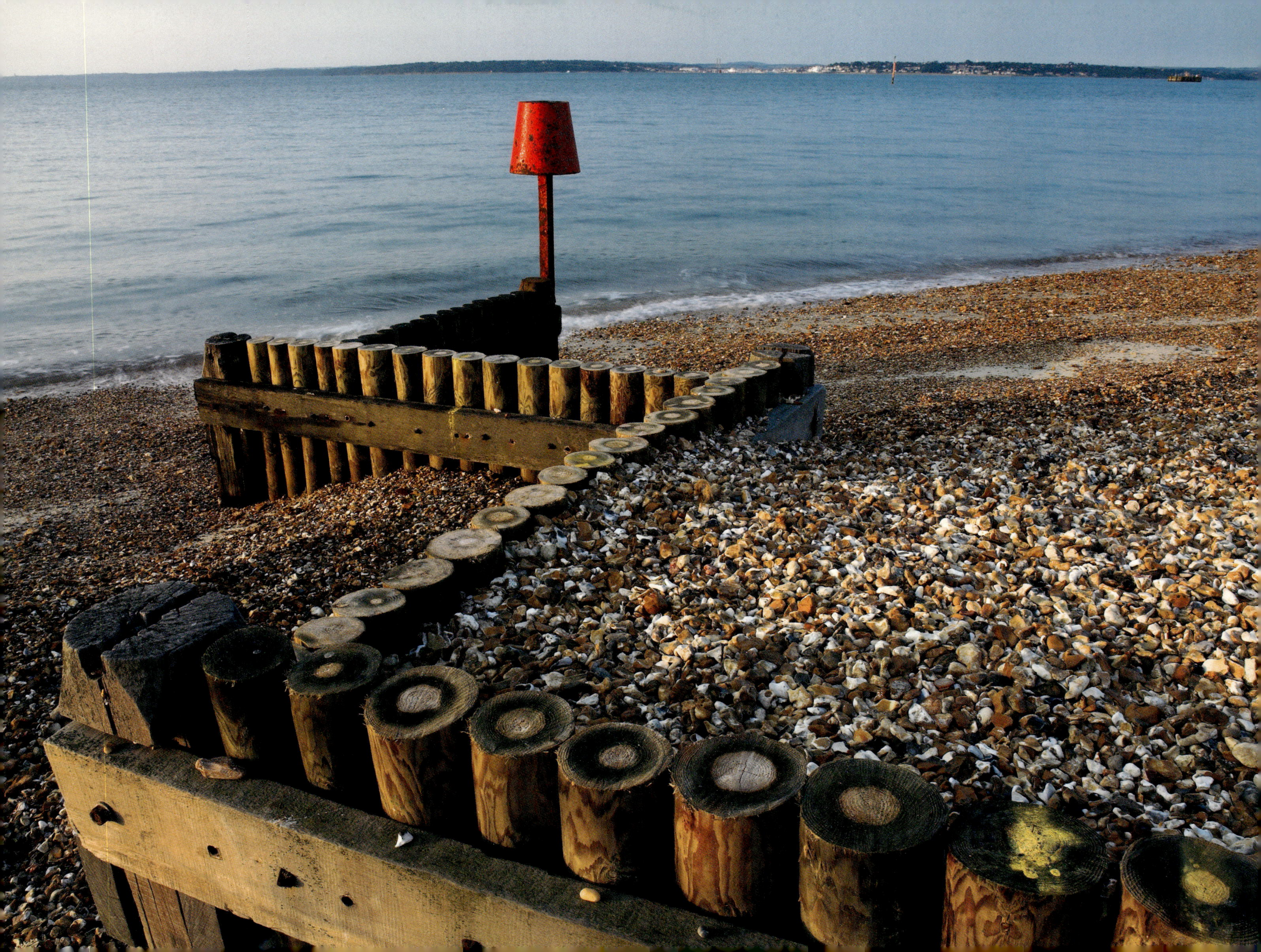

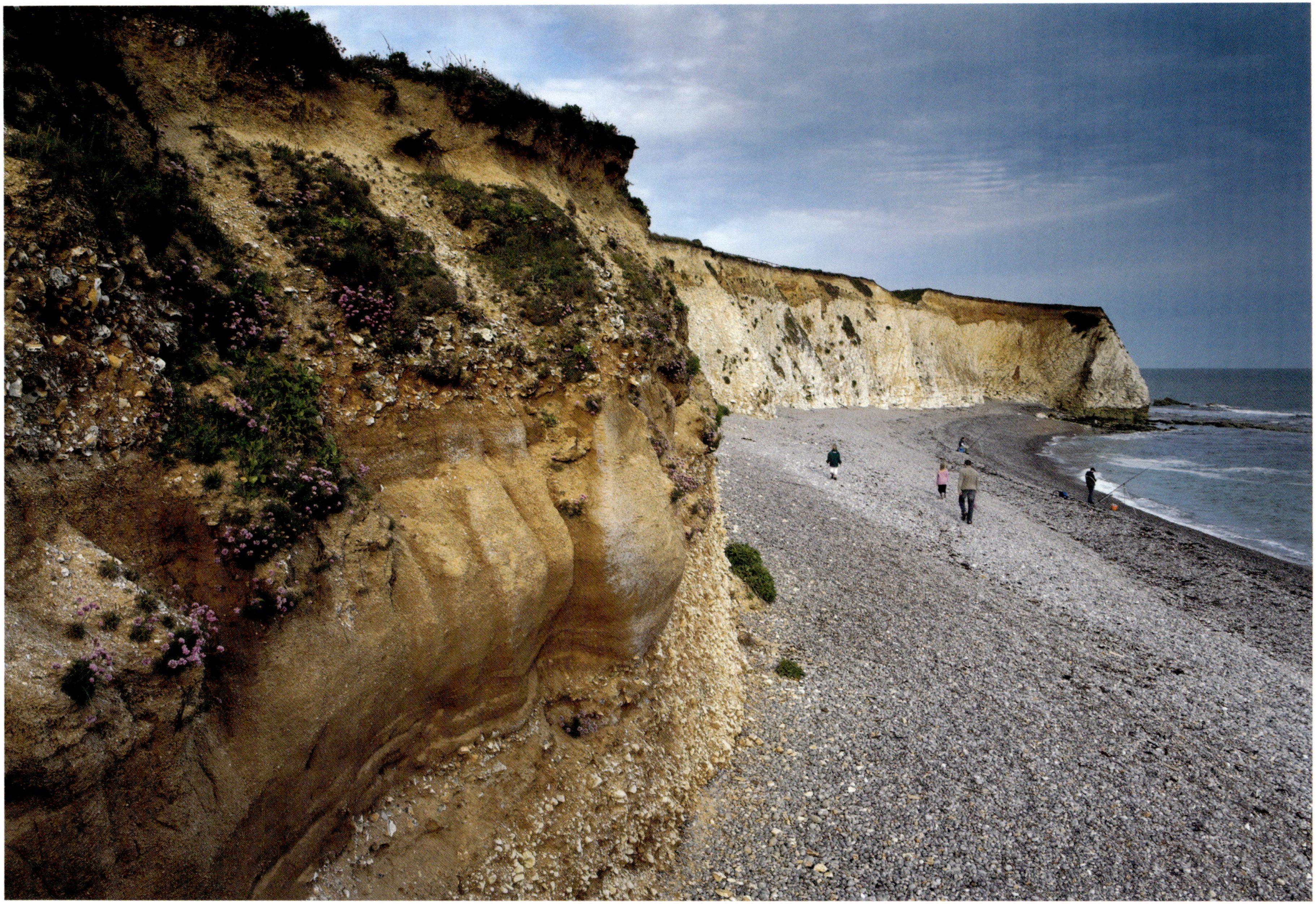

The rugged cliffs at Freshwater Bay, on the west coast of the Isle of Wight

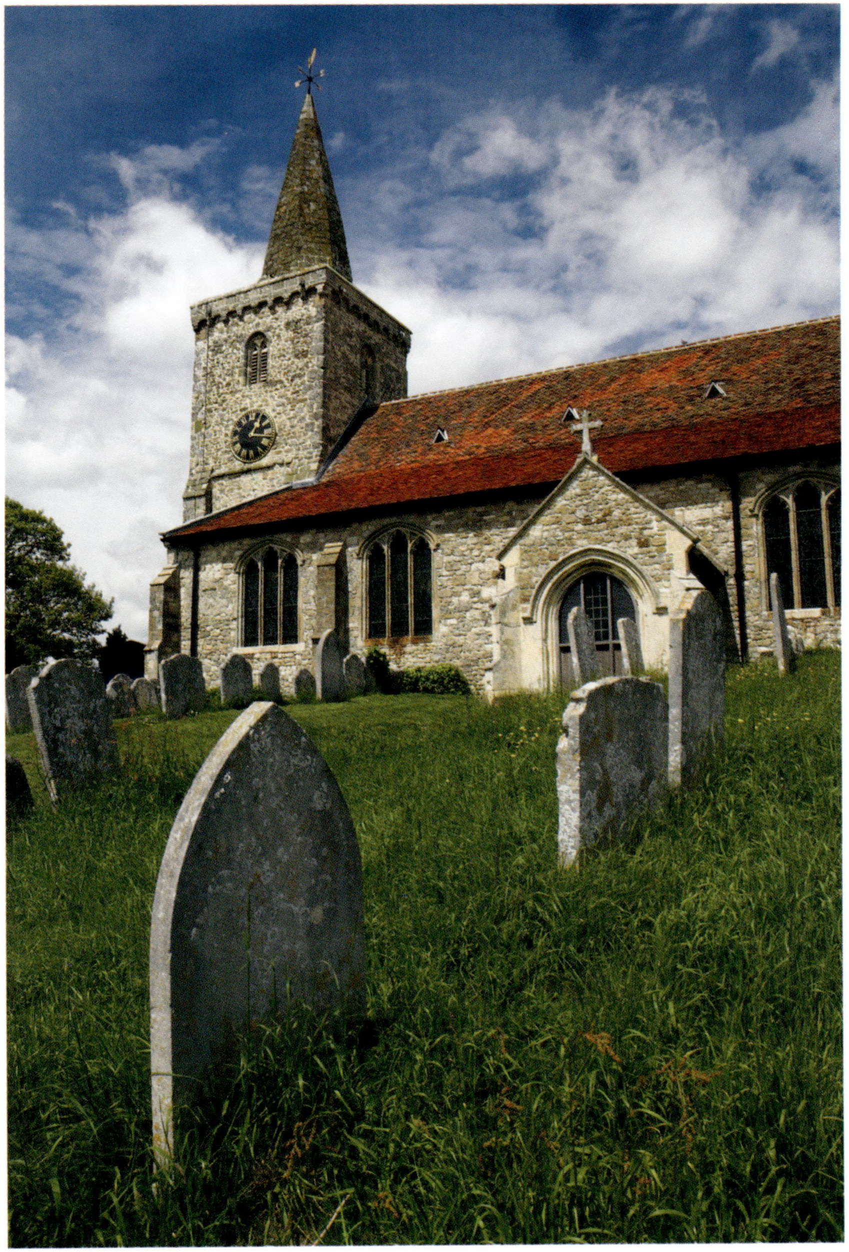

The 12th-century Brading Parish Church on the Isle of Wight

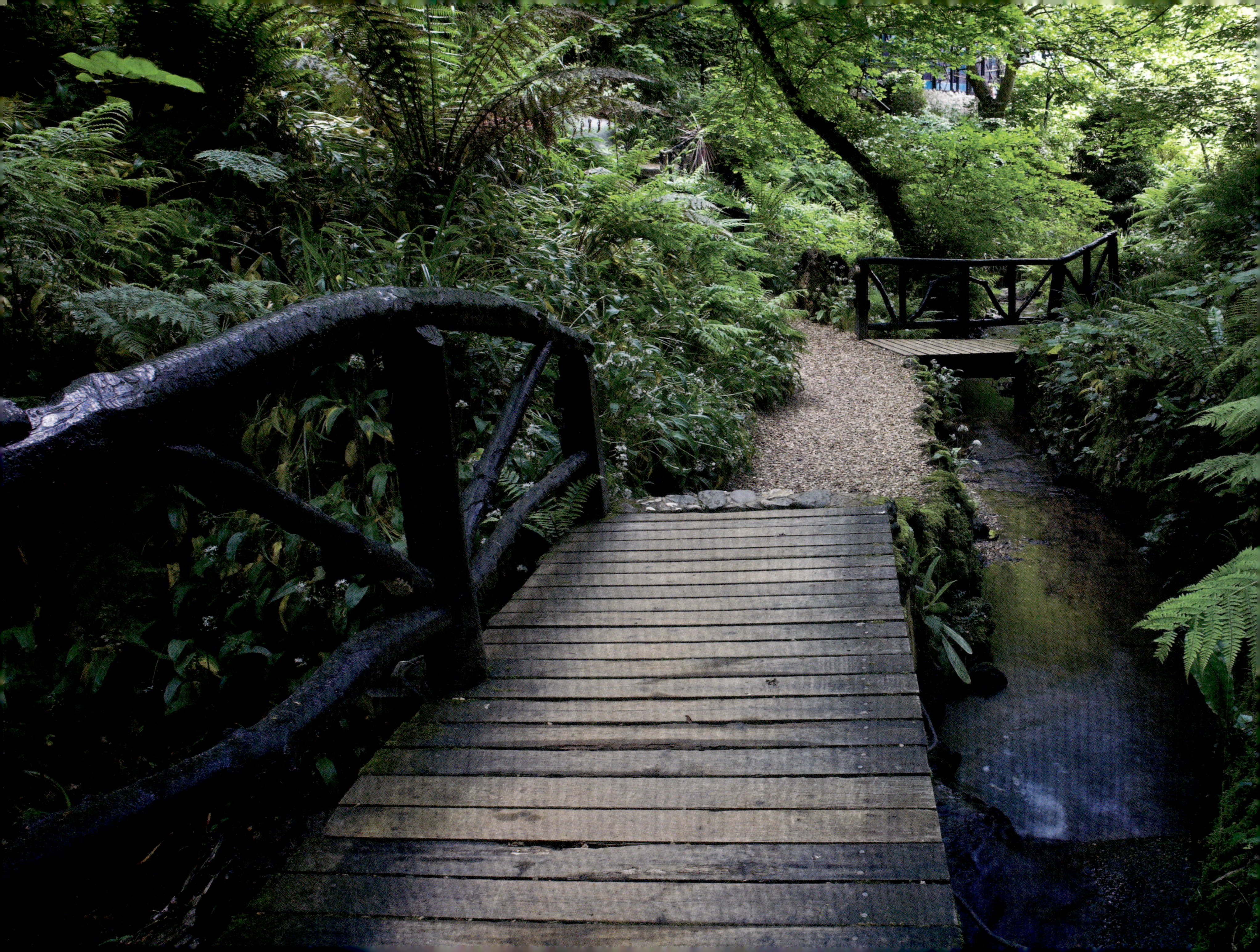

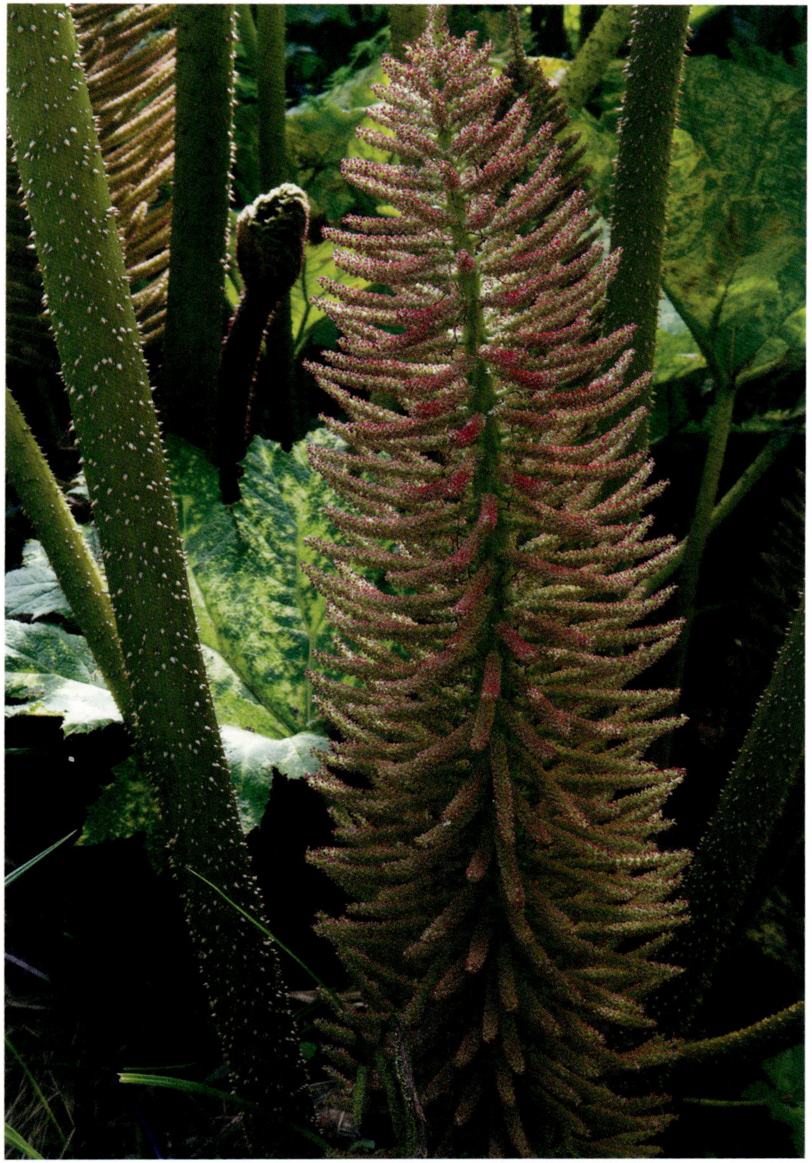

The flower of a tropical gunnera plant, Shanklin Chine, Isle of Wight
Opposite: Wooden walkways pass over the small stream at Shanklin

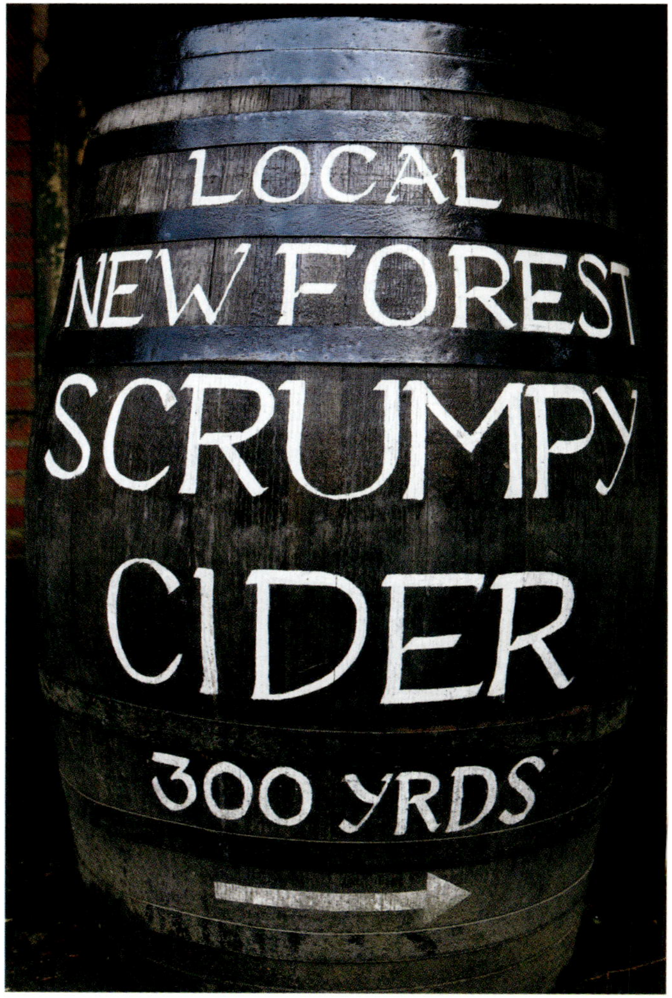

Barrel advertising local New Forest Scrumpy Cider at Burley

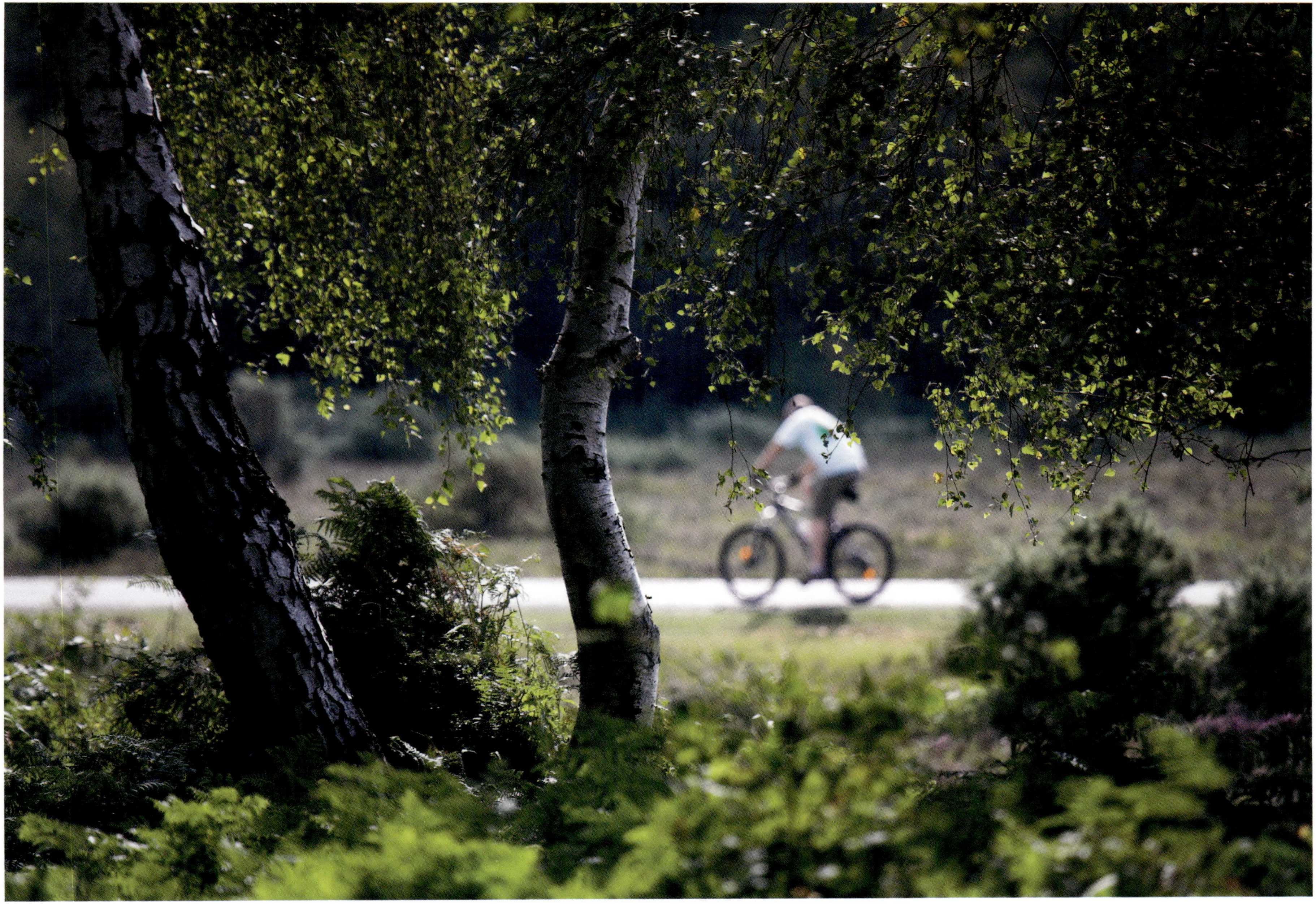

A lone cyclist blazes a trail through the trees near Ipley, New Forest

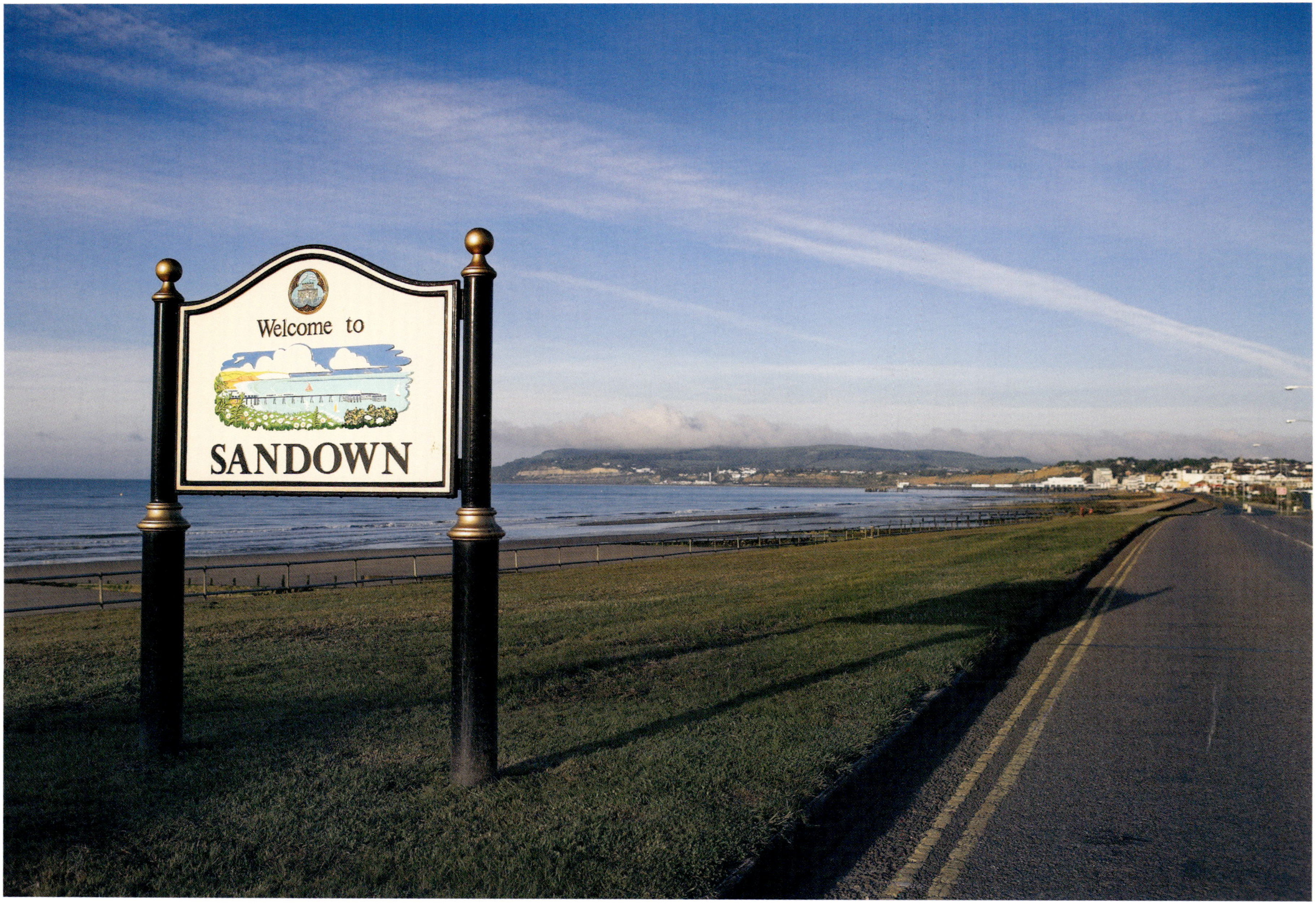

Sandown town sign overlooking Sandown Bay, Isle of Wight

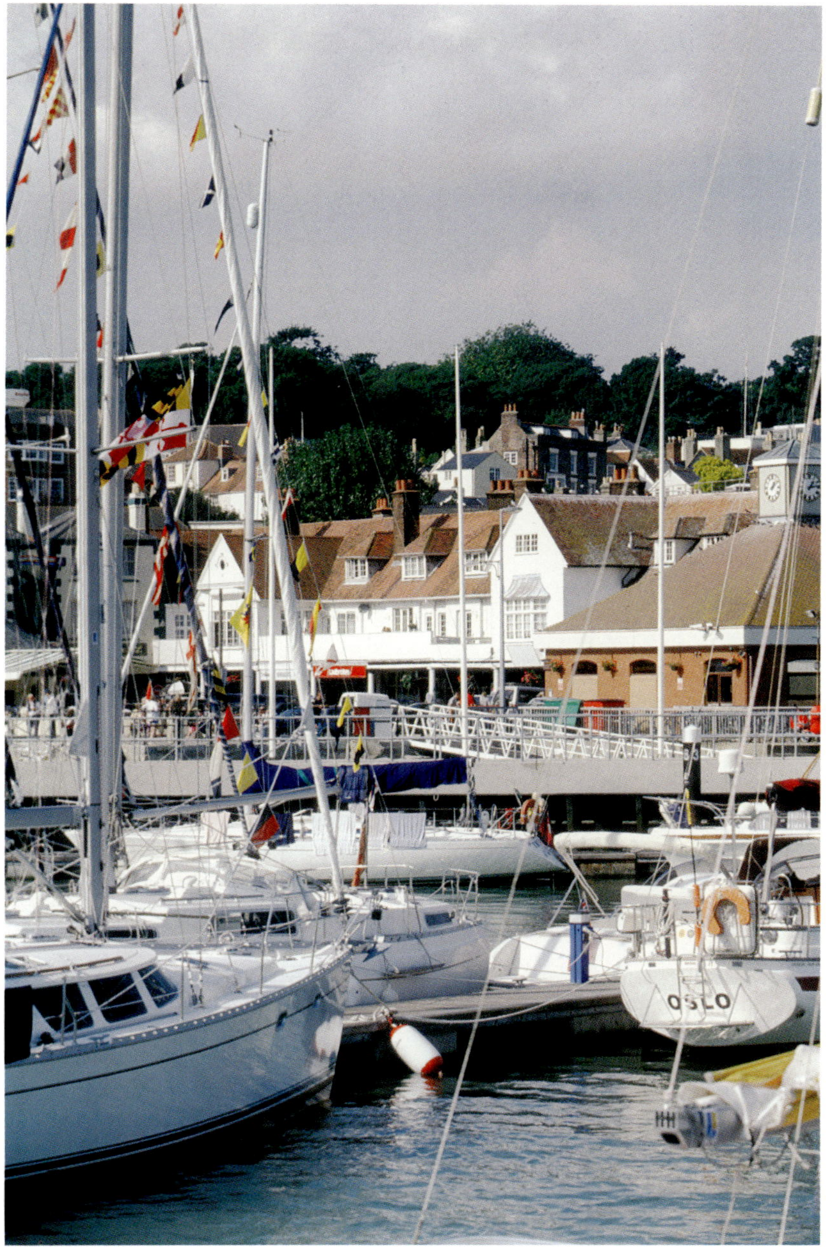

Boats in the harbour at Cowes on the Isle of Wight

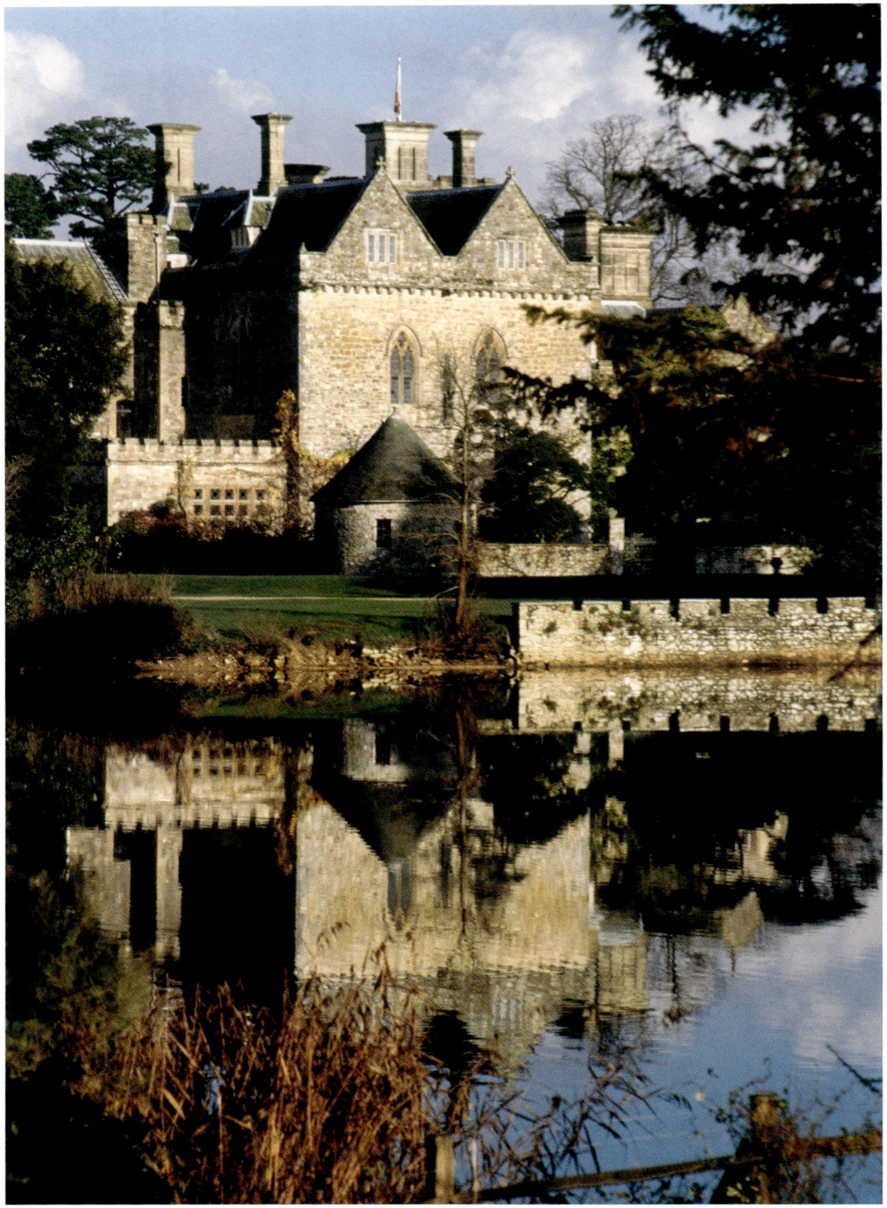

Beaulieu's Palace House set in glorious grounds reflected in the Beaulieu River, New Forest. In part dating to the 14th century, it is a family home still lived in by the present Lord Montagu and his family

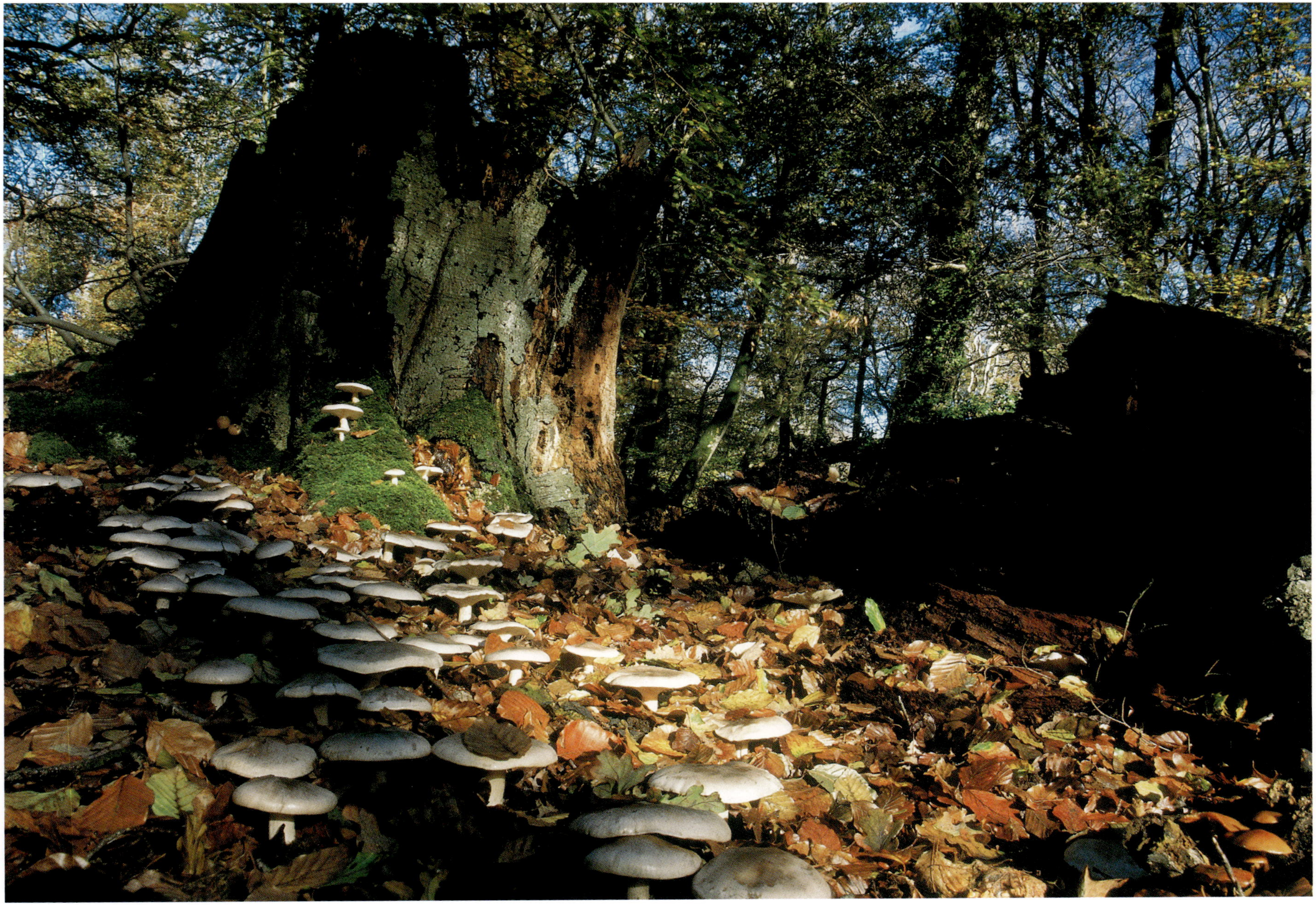

Autumnal fungi in the undergrowth, New Forest

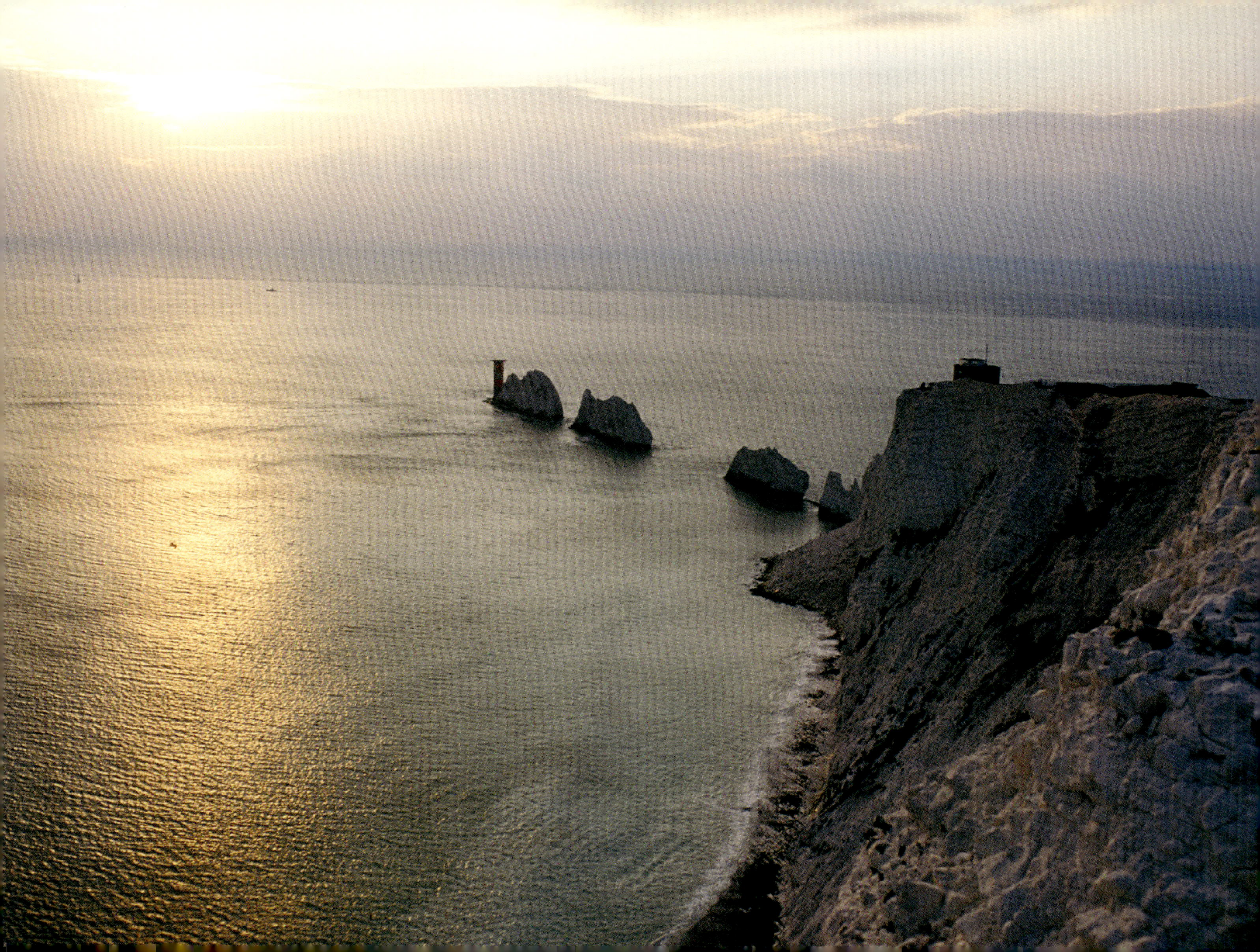

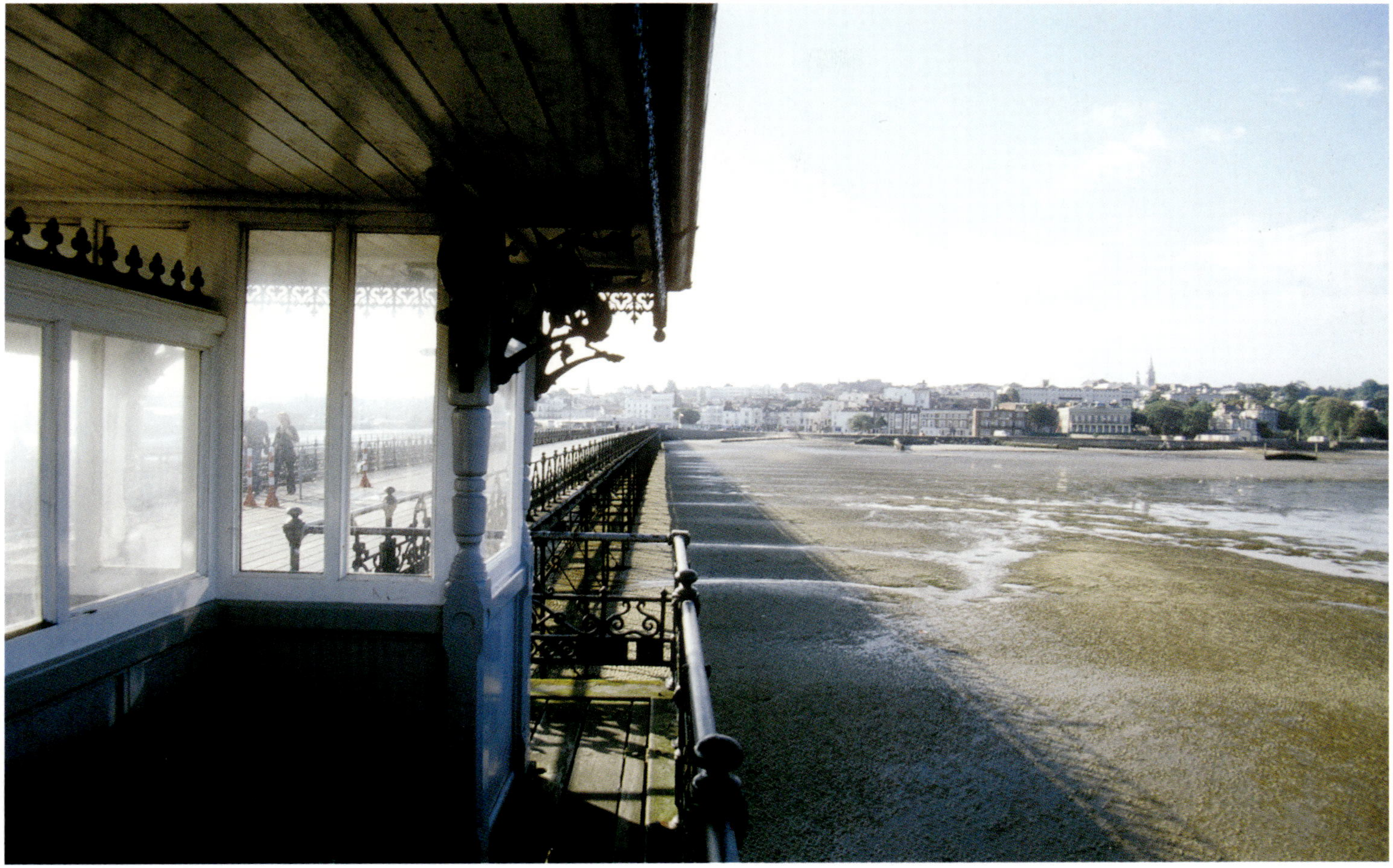

Looking down the length of Ryde Pier on the Isle of Wight
Opposite: Sunset view of the Needles on the Isle of Wight and lighthouse from the clifftop

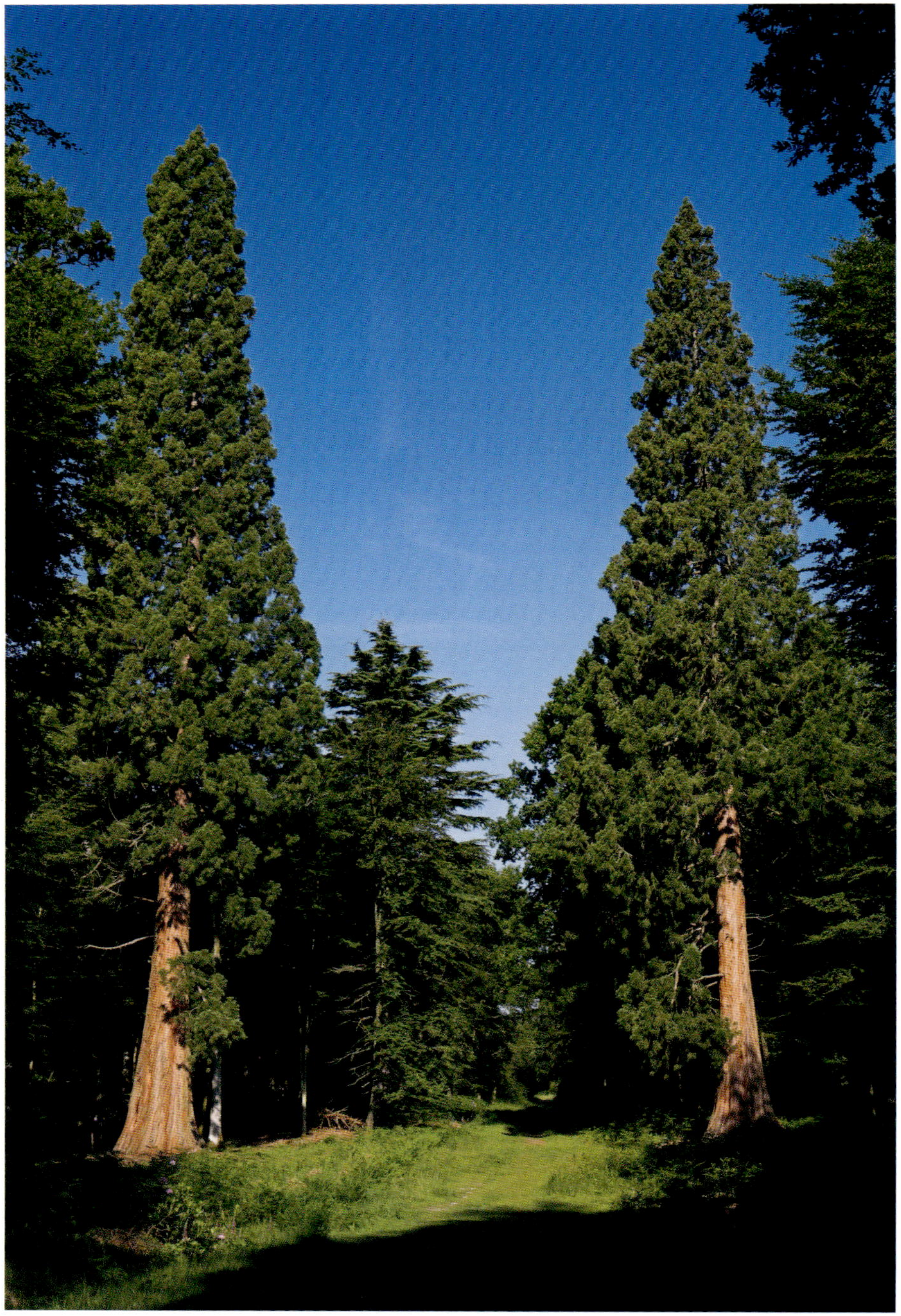

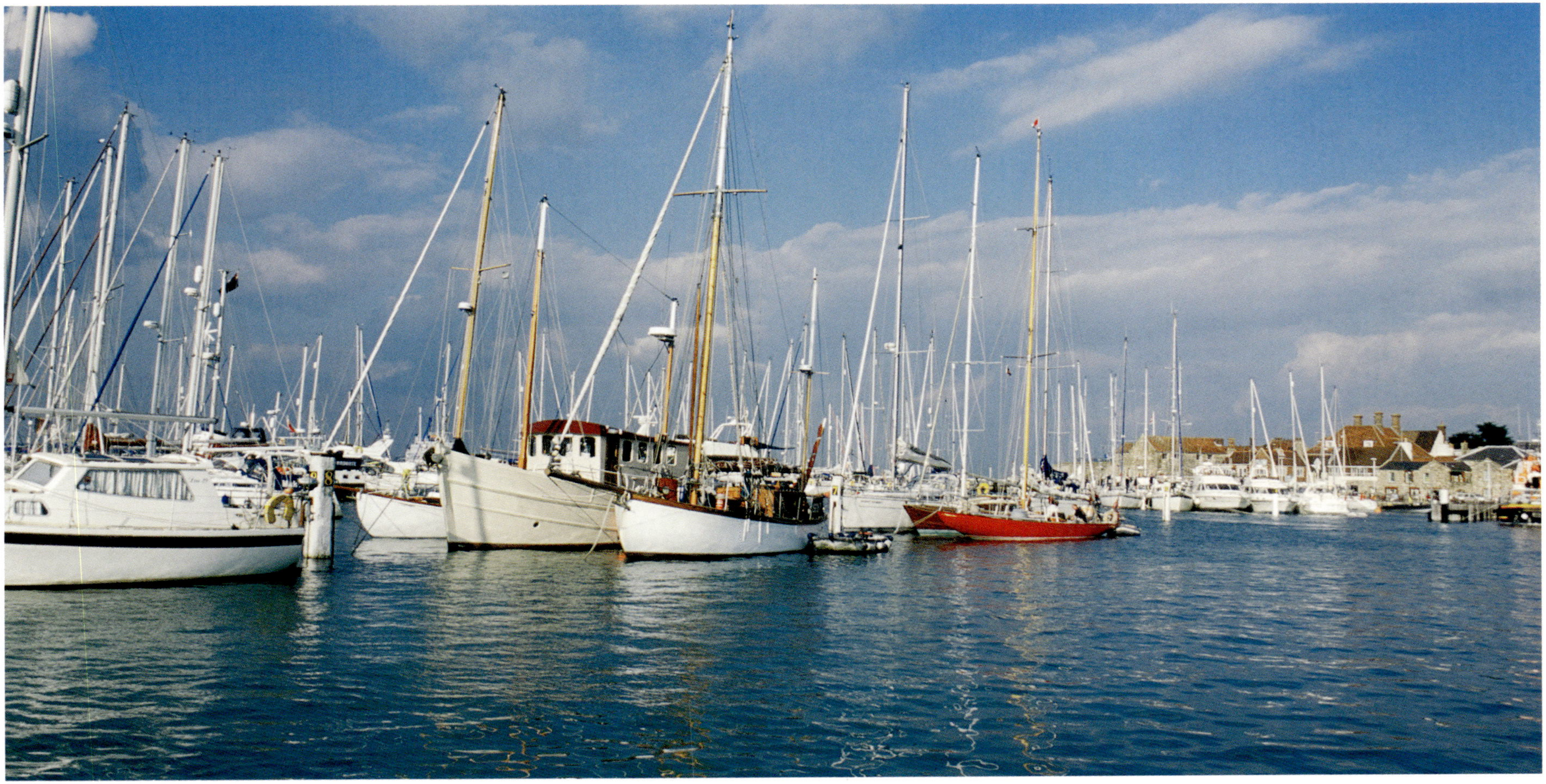

Boats in the harbour at Yarmouth on the Isle of Wight

Opposite: The giant sequoias on the Tall Trees Trail, Rhinefield Ornamental Drive in the New Forest

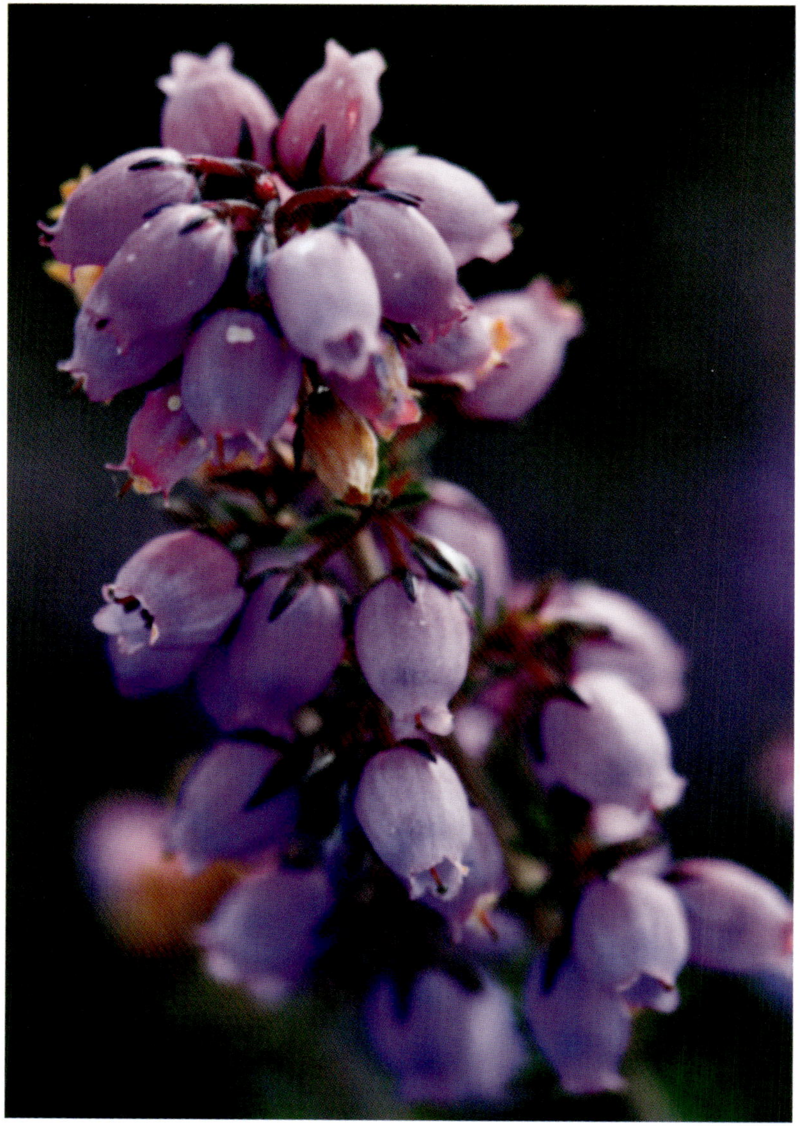

Detail of bell heather which grows profusely on the heathland in the New Forest
Opposite: Rolling heathland carpeted in heather and bracken at Rockford Common, near Ringwood, New Forest

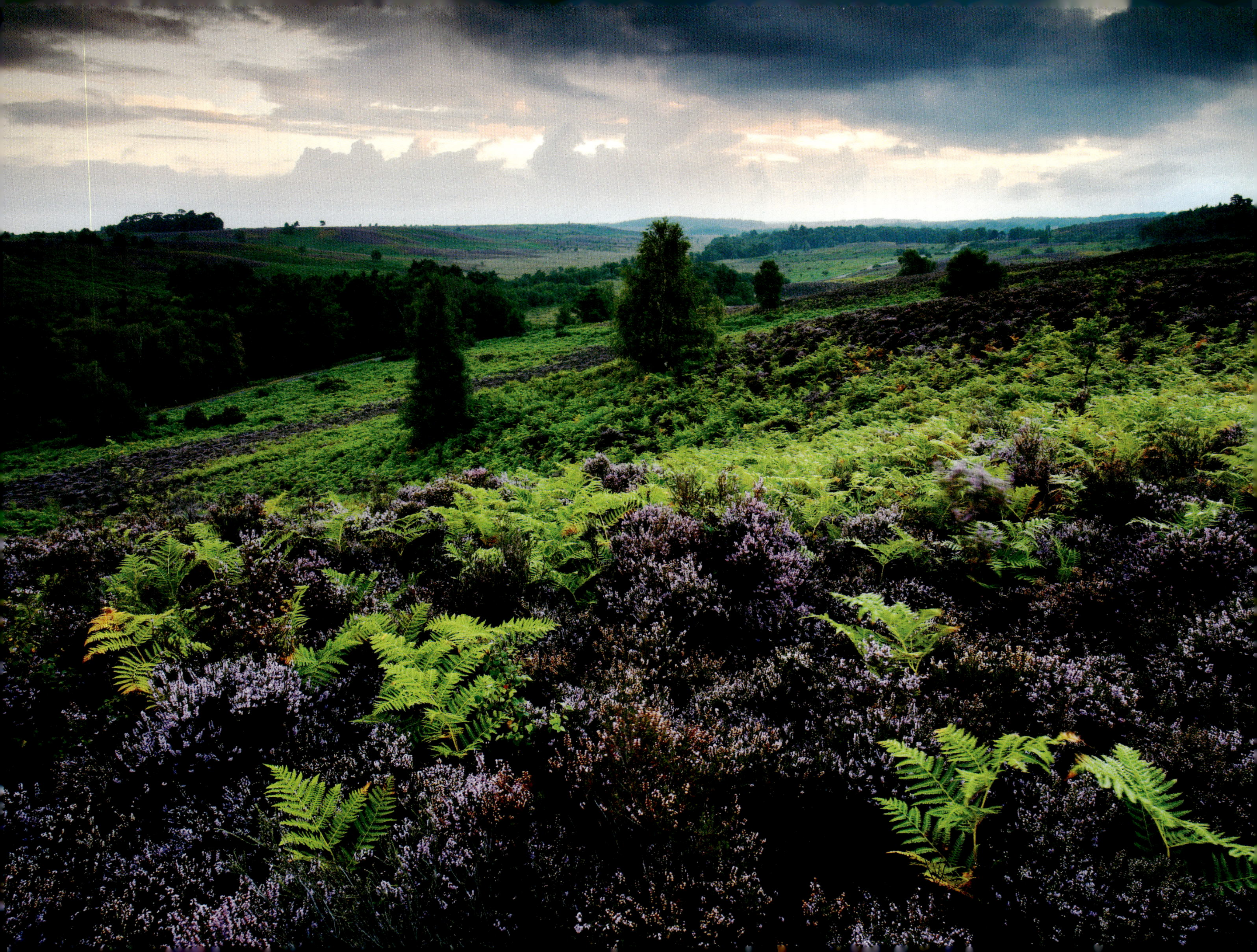

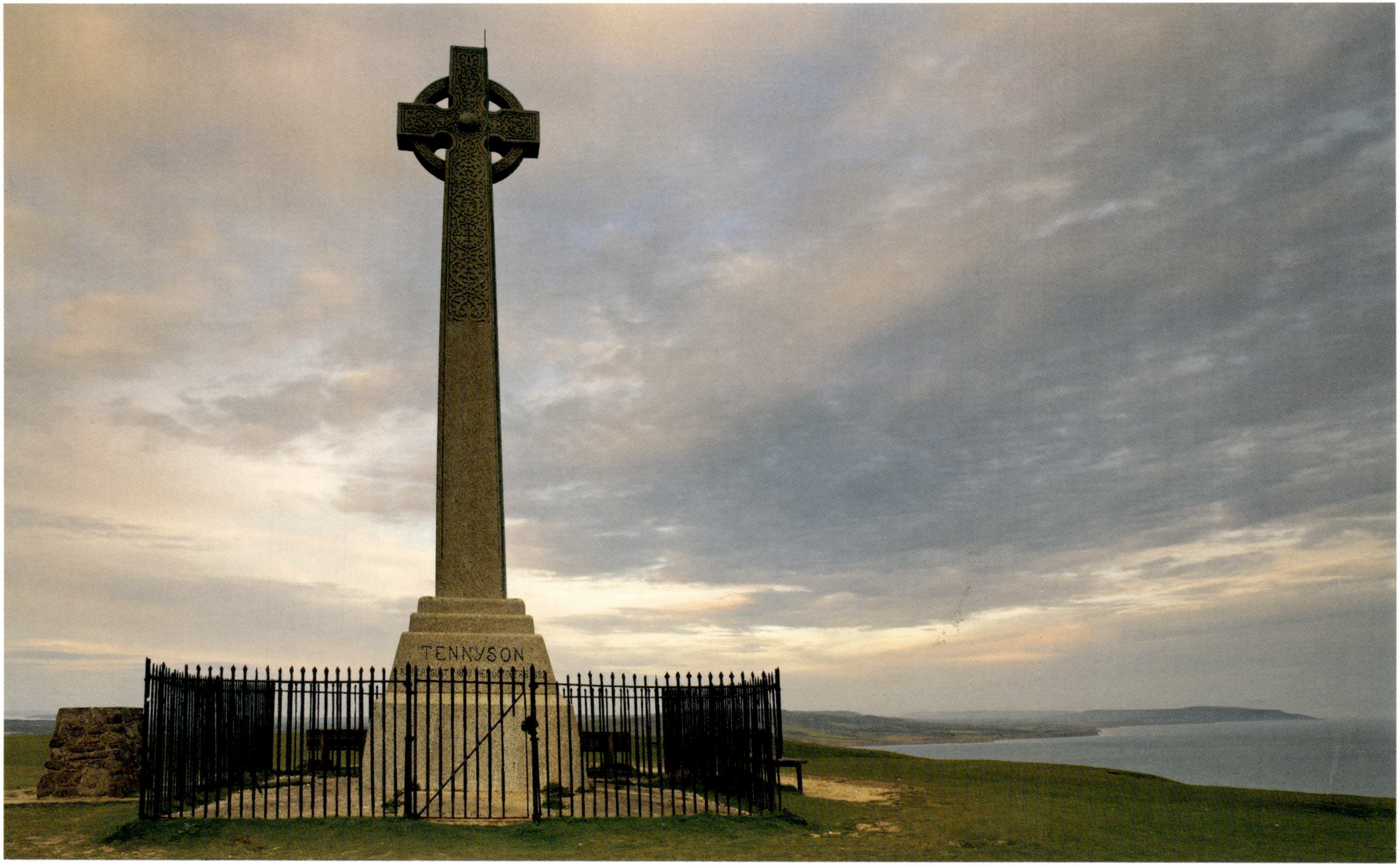

Freshwater Bay, Tennyson's monument on the crest of Tennyson Down, with sweeping views over the south coast of the Isle of Wight
Opposite: The incoming tide surges around the weather-beaten chalk cliffs at Freshwater Bay

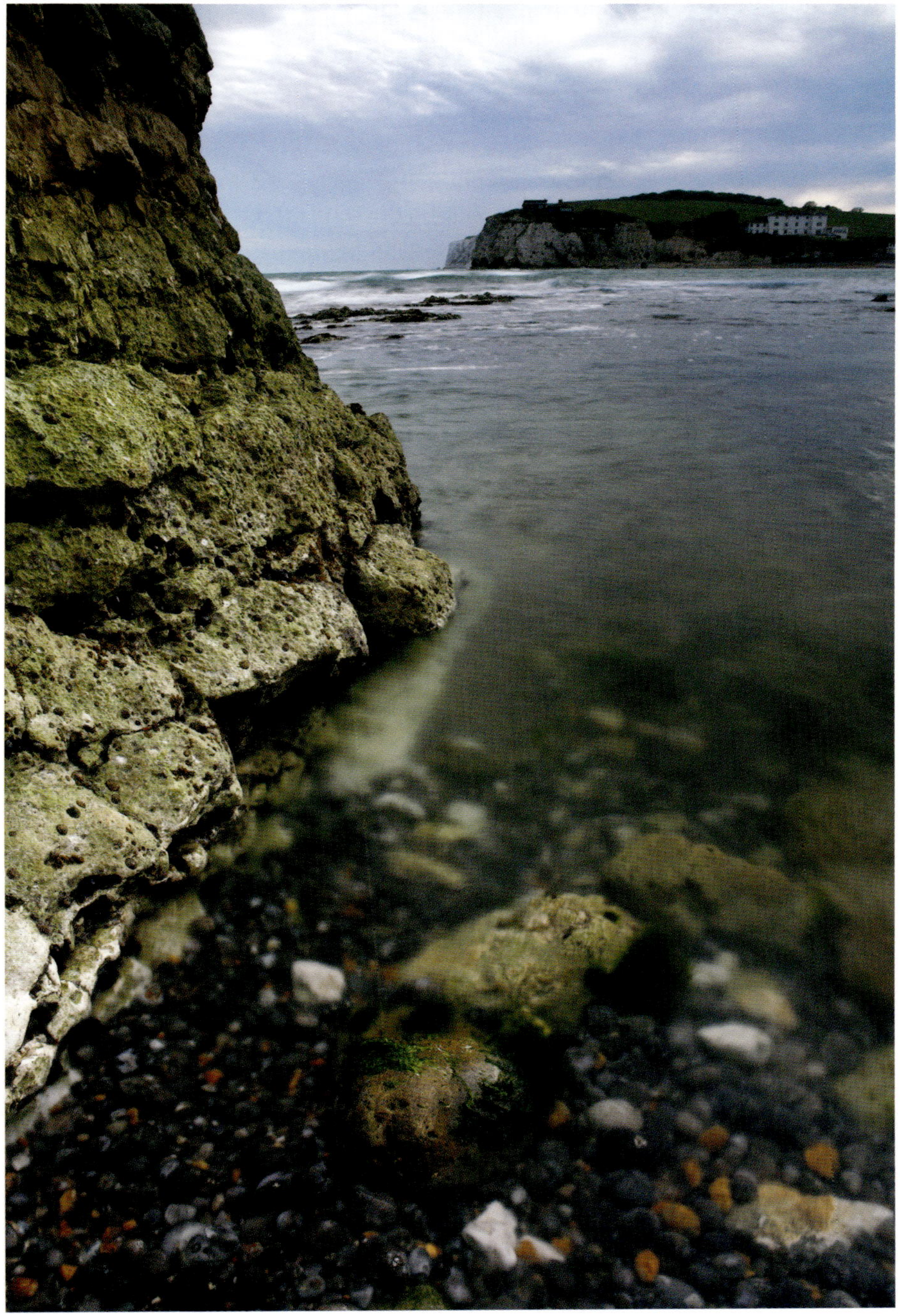

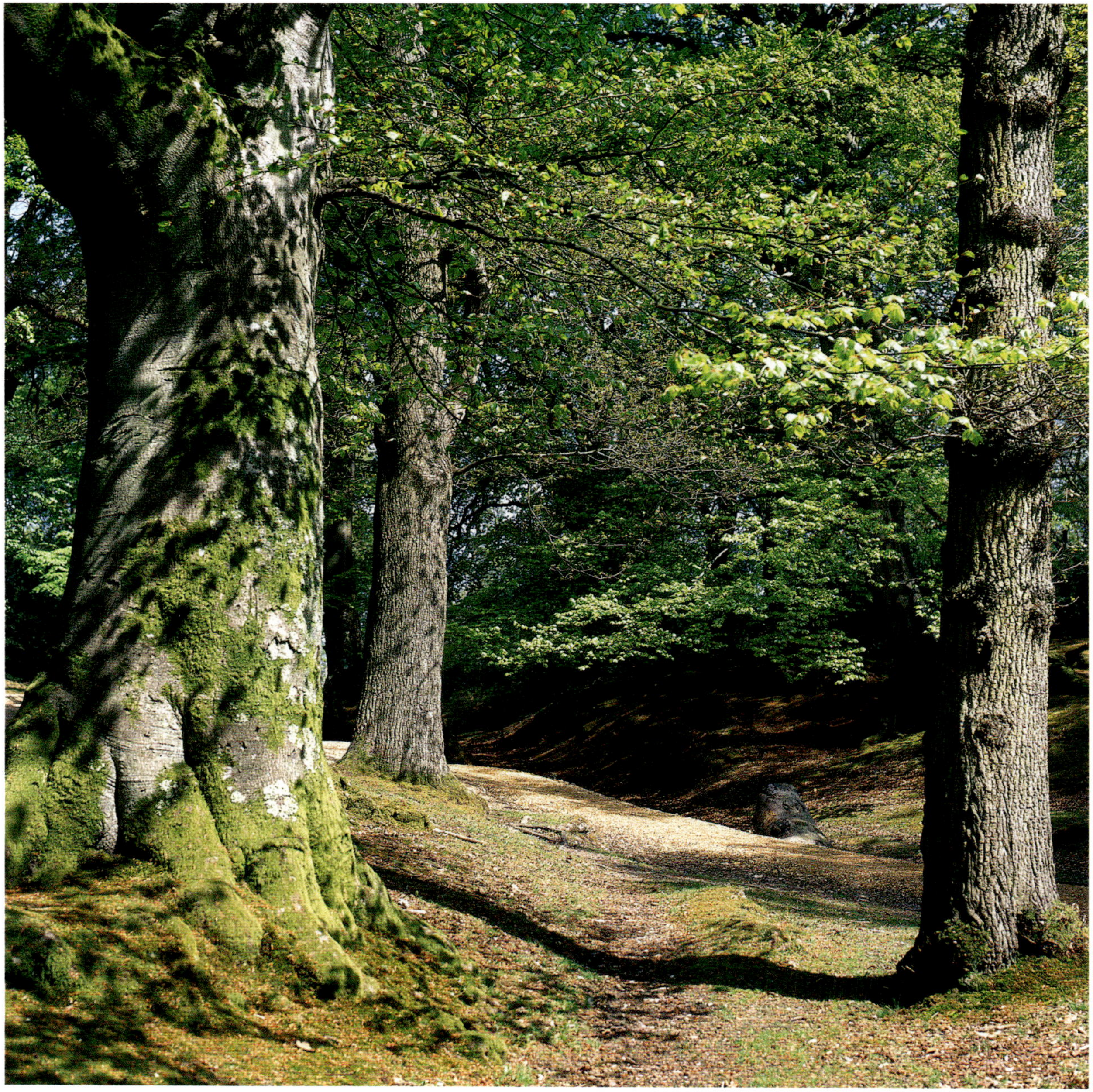

A path through the New Forest in Burley

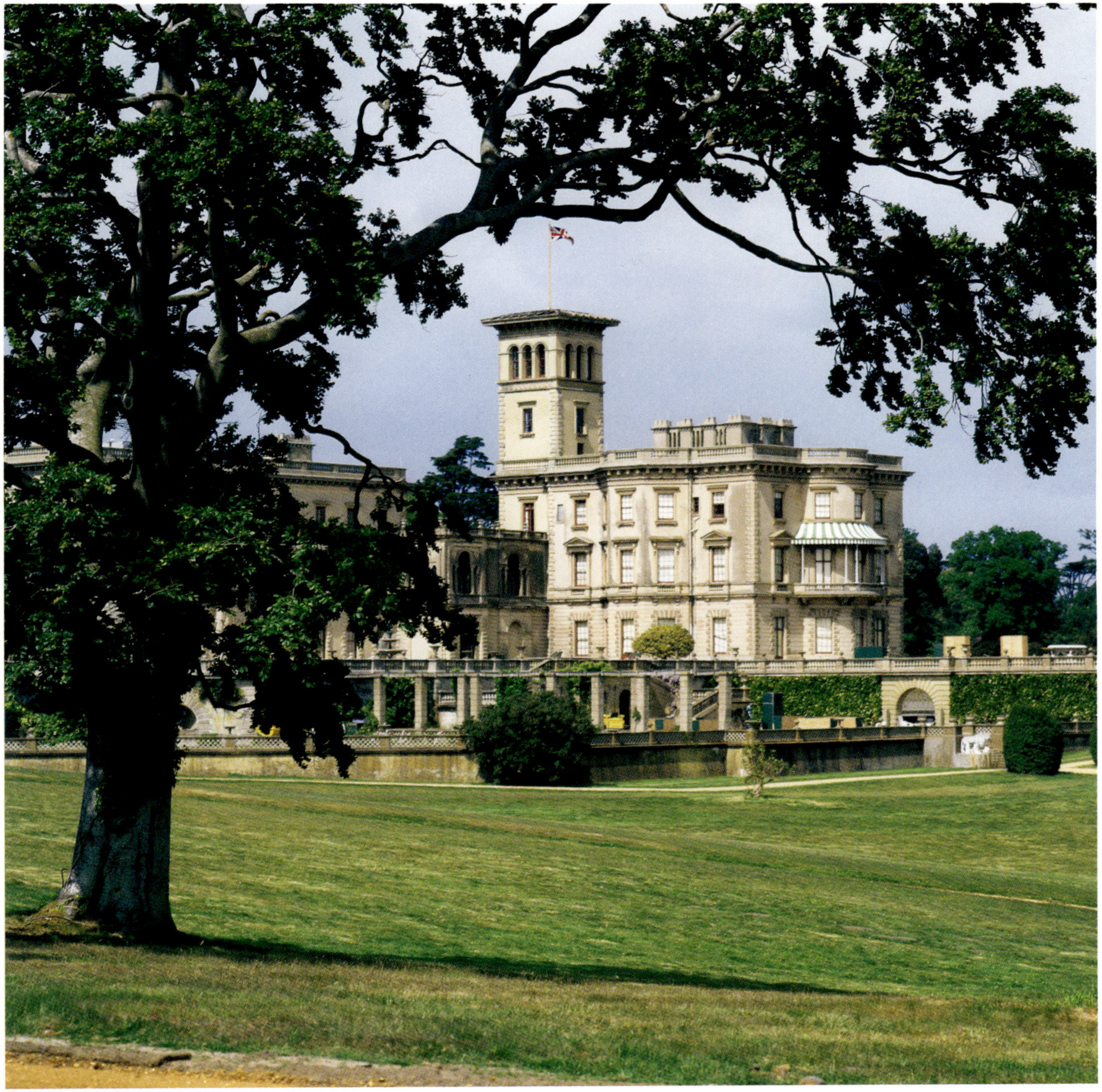

Osborne House - which was designed by Prince Albert and Thomas Cubitt in the style of an Italian villa. Queen Victoria died here in her Isle of Wight home in 1901

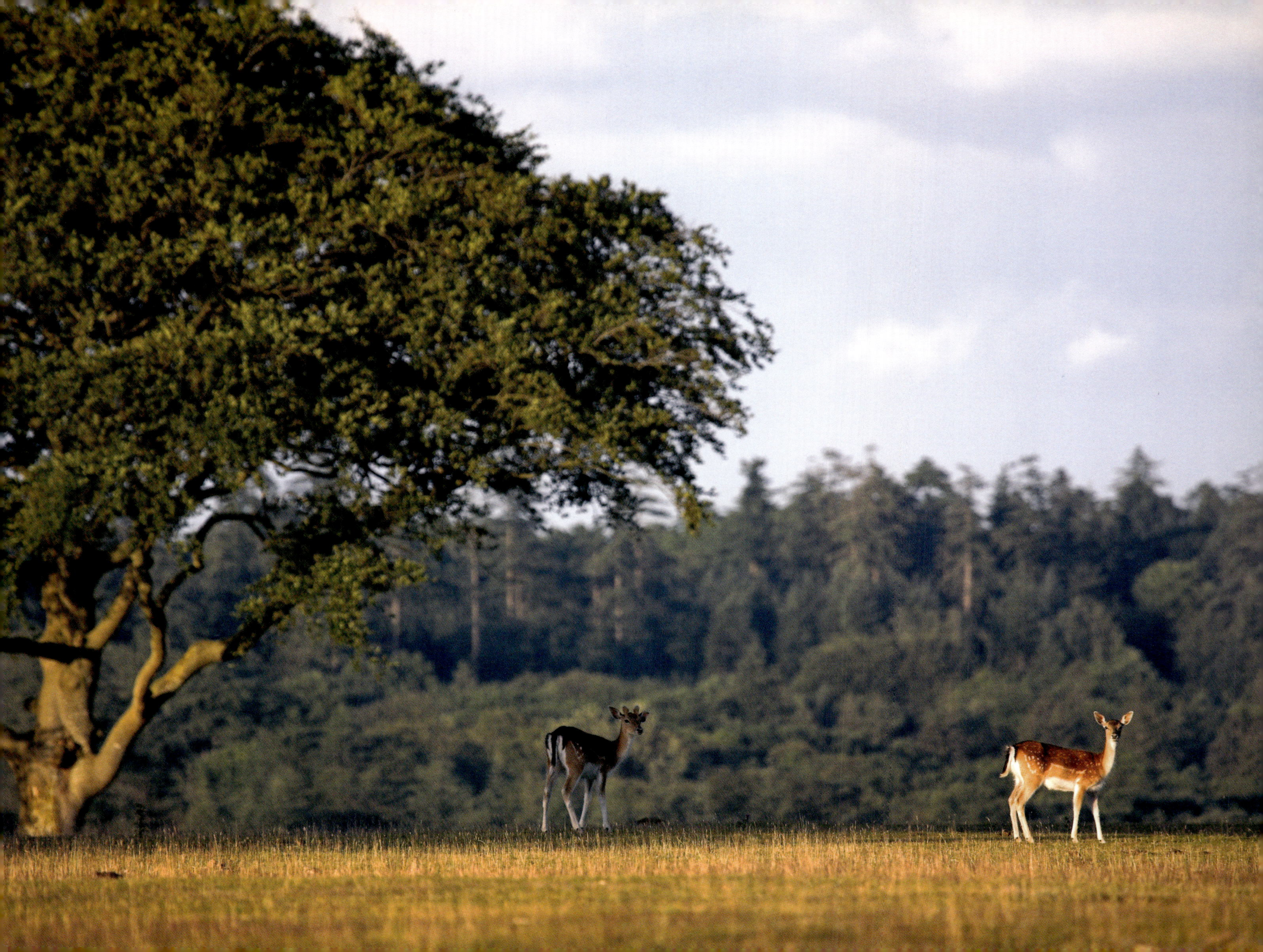

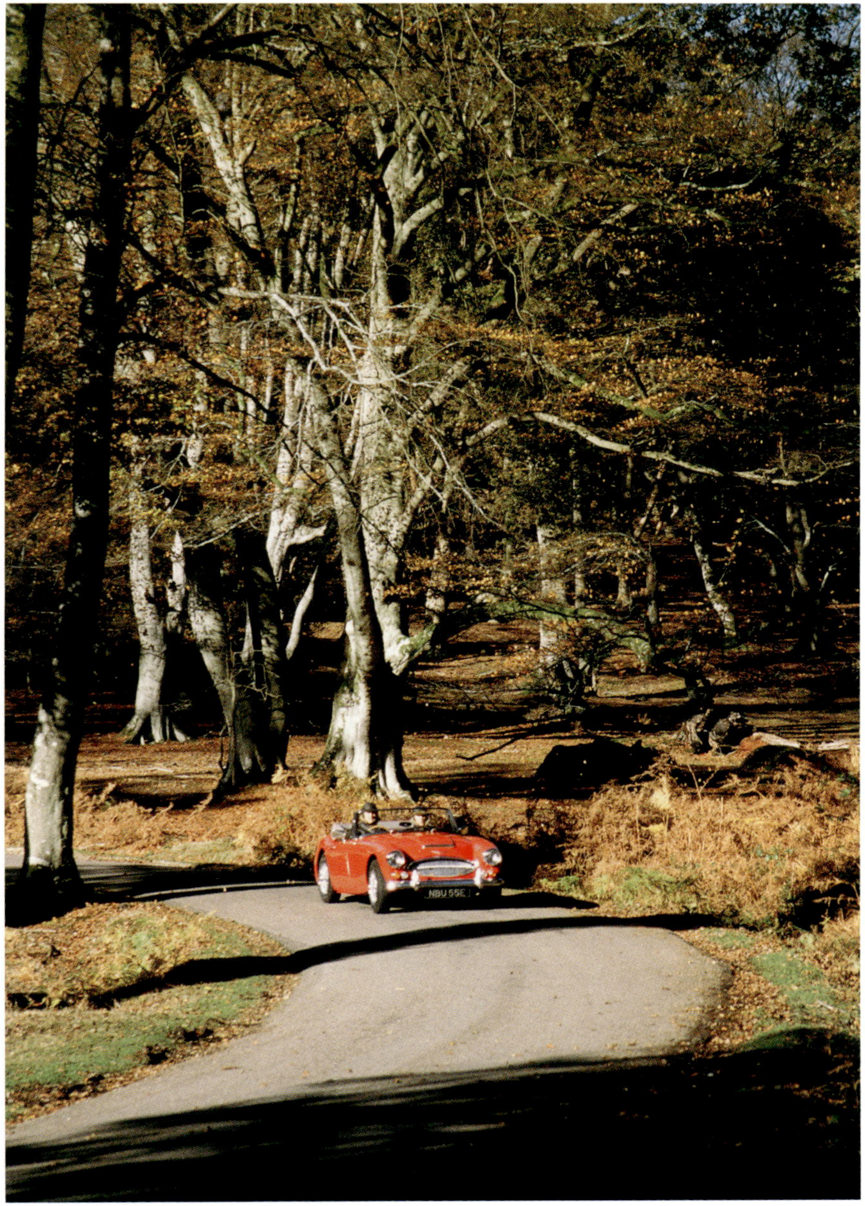

Austin Healey 3000 travelling along the northern side of the Ornamental Drive in the New Forest
Opposite: Two fallow deer graze on the plains near Stoney Cross, Isle of Wight

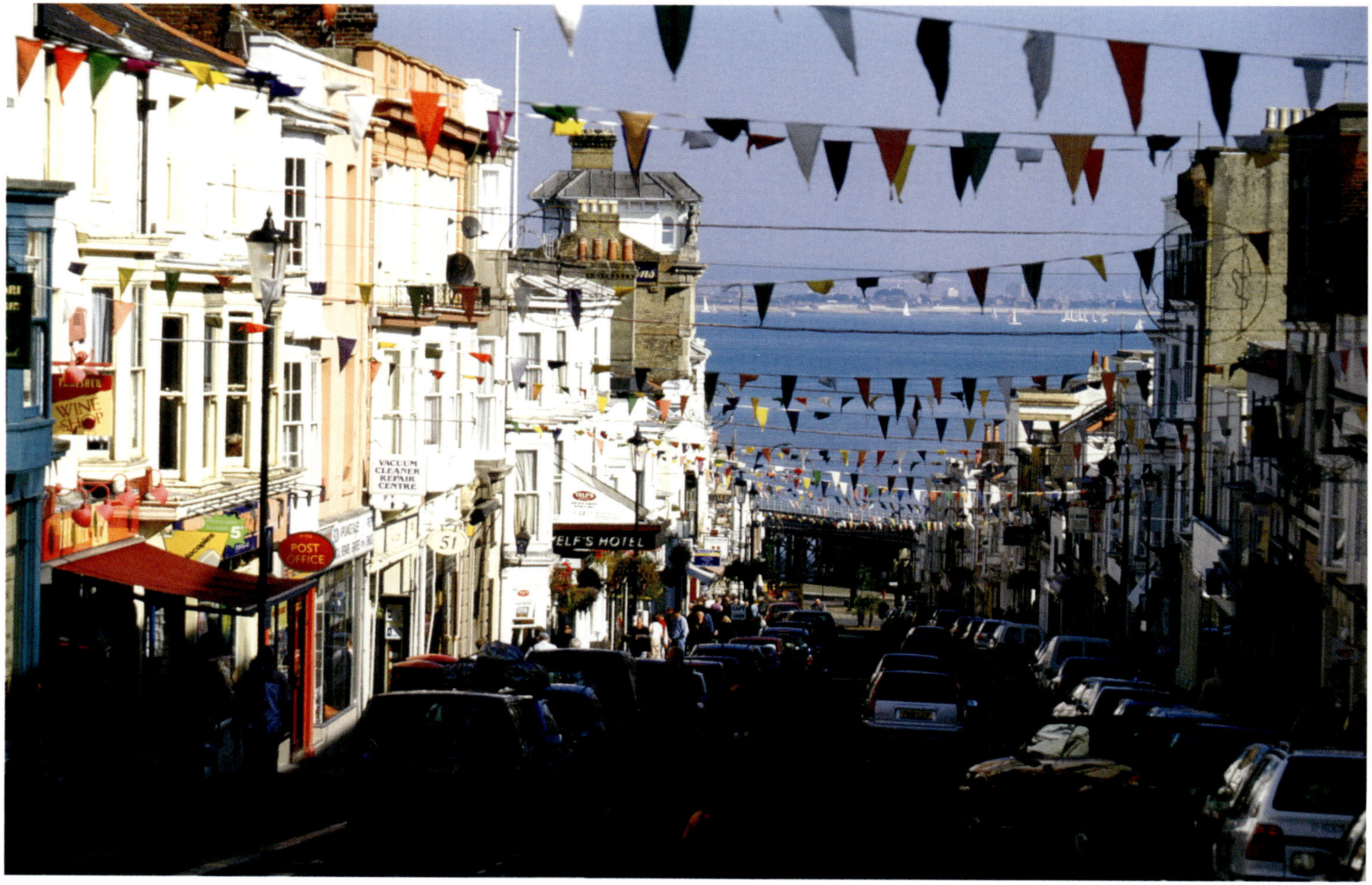

Festival bunting on the High Street at Ryde, Isle of Wight.

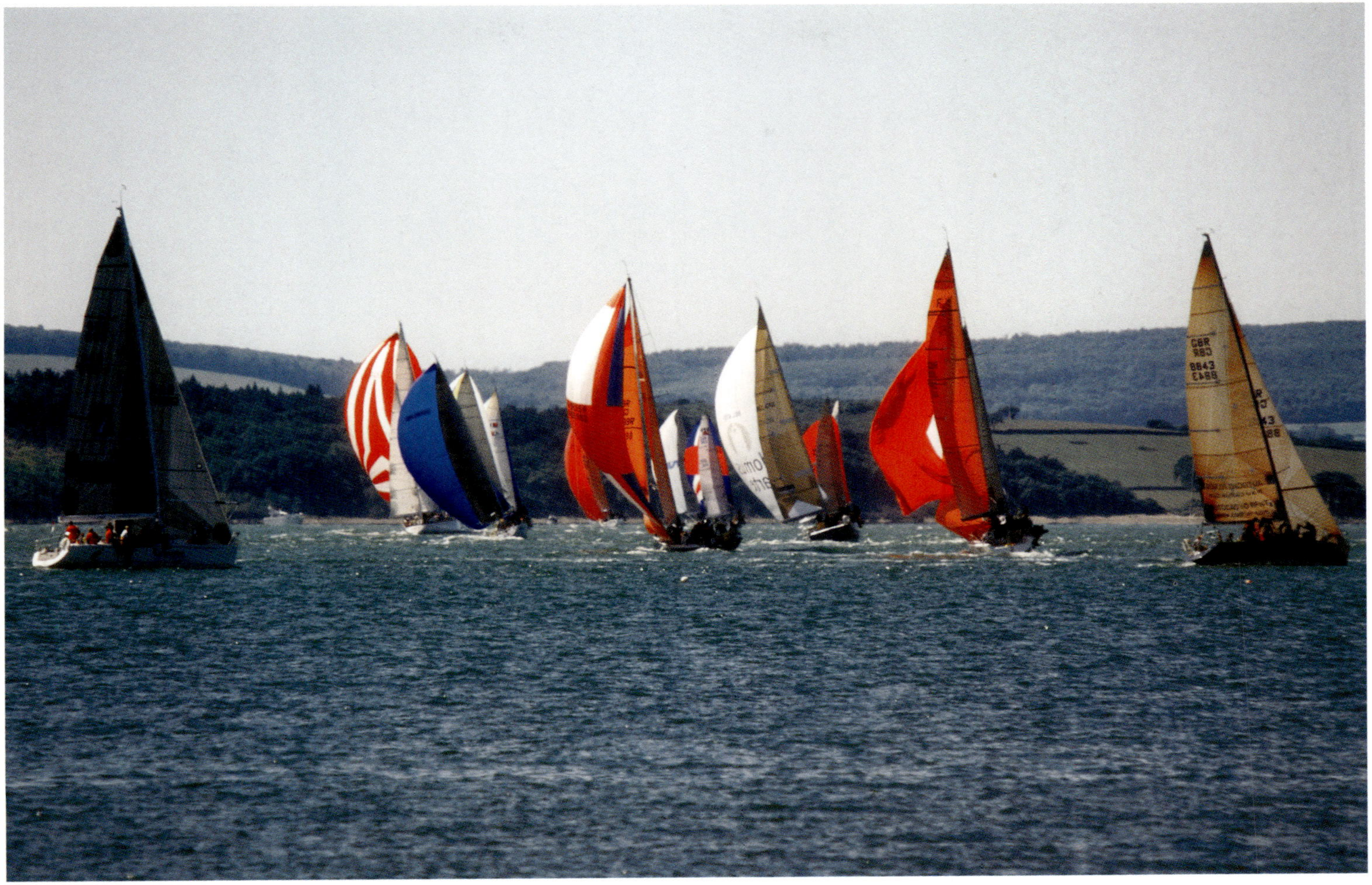

Sailing boats racing during Cowes Week, Isle of Wight

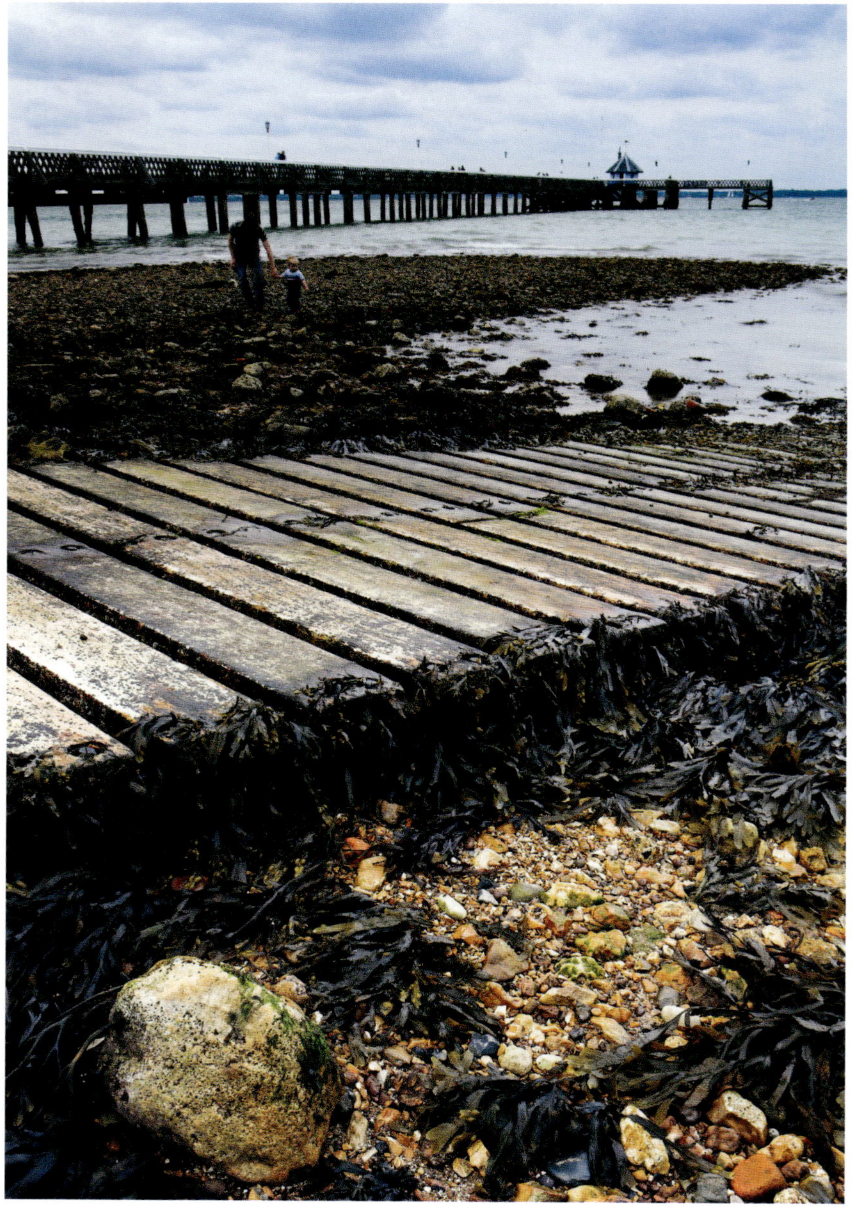

Father and son at Yarmouth waterfront with the pier in the background
Opposite: A view across Freshwater Bay to the hotels and Tennyson Down beyond, Isle of Wight

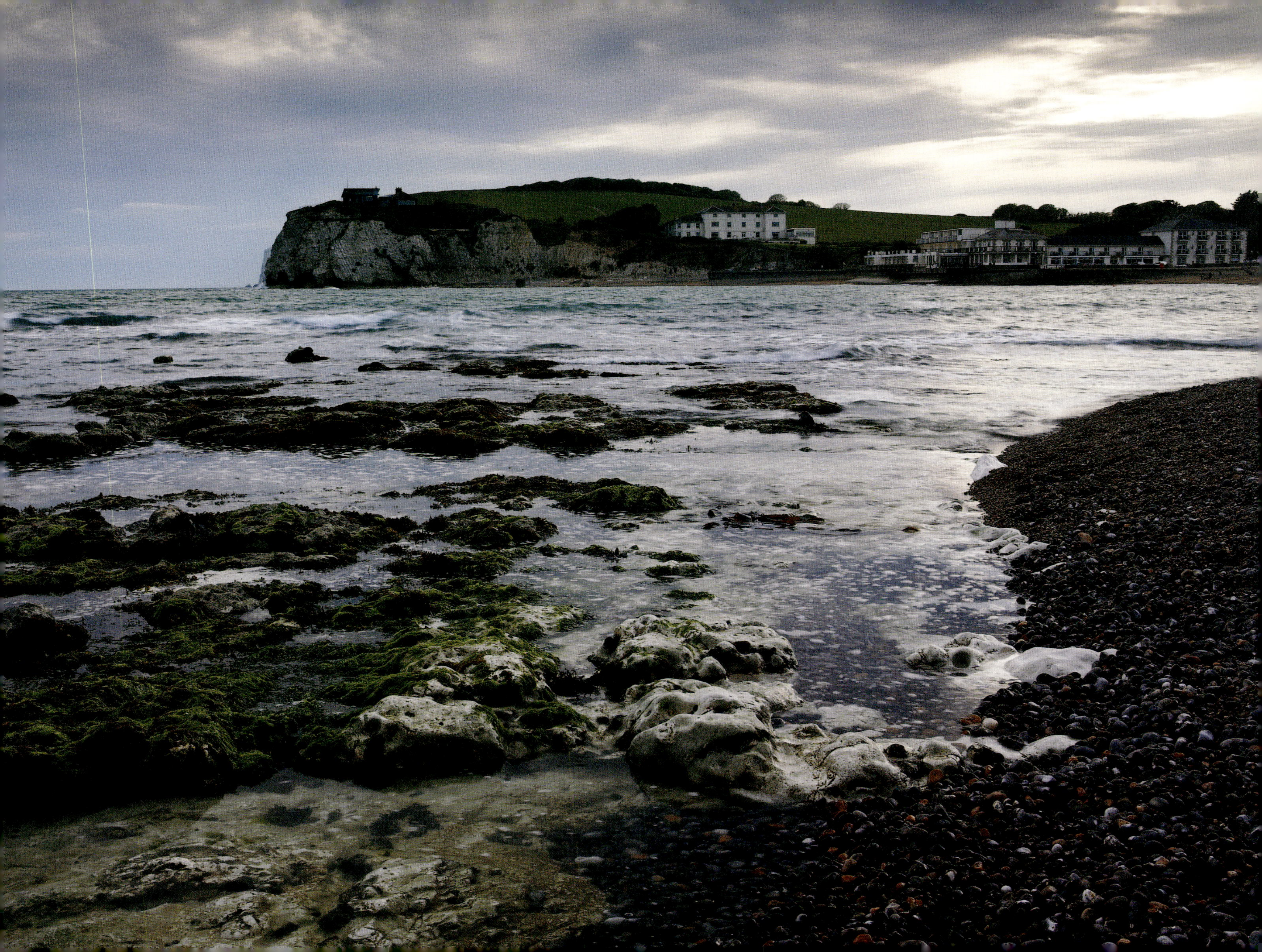

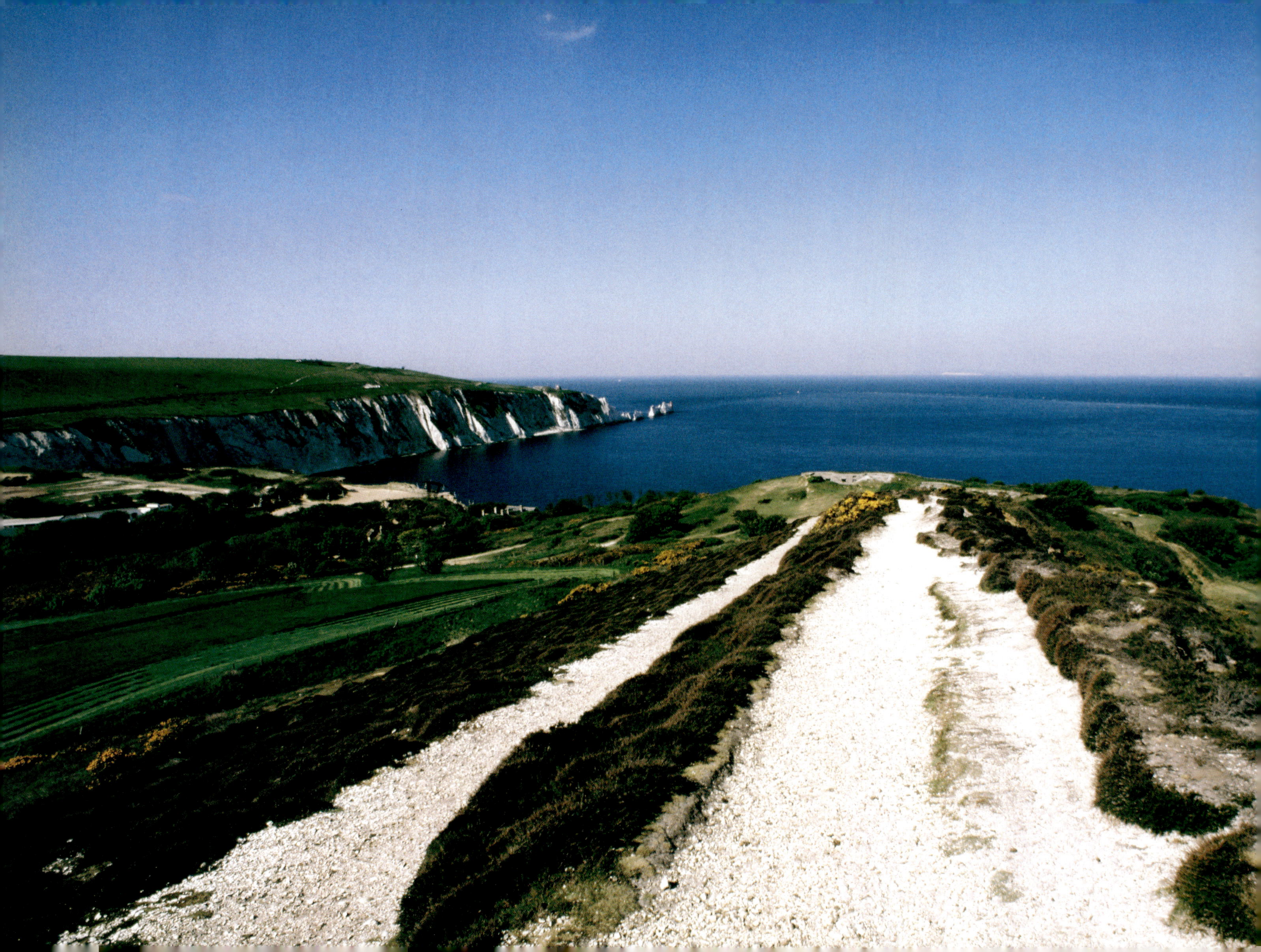

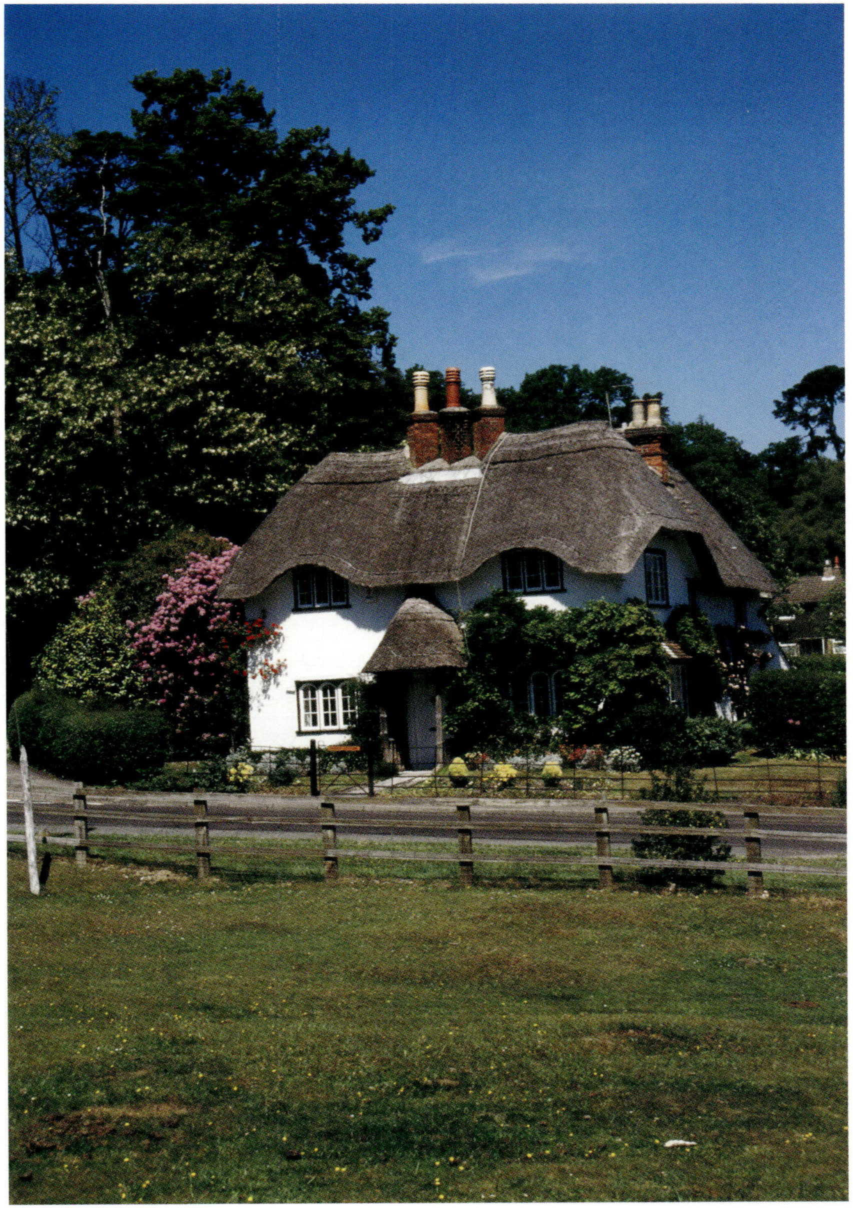

A thatched cottage with flower-filled garden at Swan Green, near Lyndhurst, in the New Forest
Opposite: Looking out over the chalk cliffs towards the Needles from Headon Warren, Alum Bay on the Isle of Wight

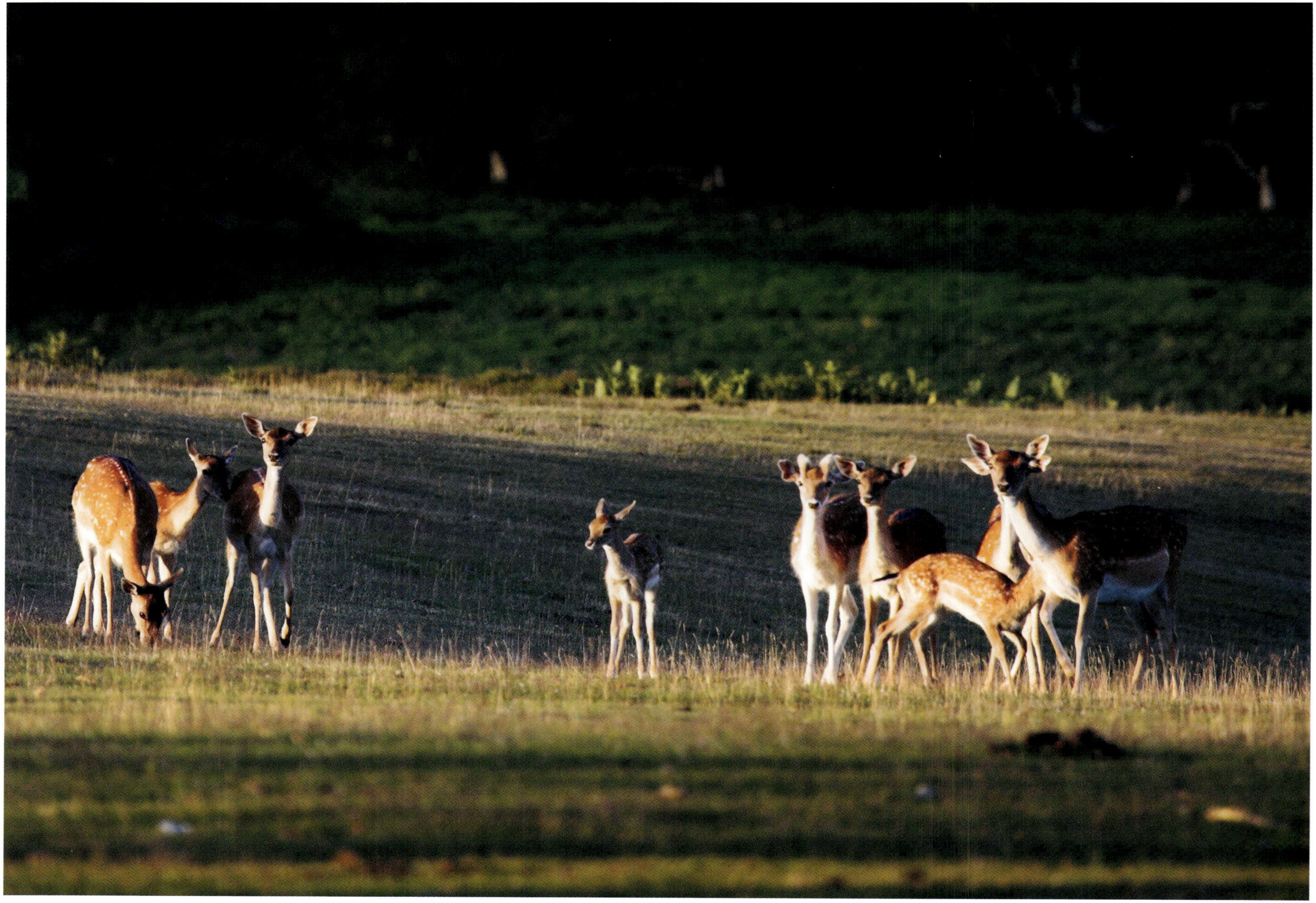

A group of fallow does and fawns graze on Backley Plain, near Burley, in the evening sunshine, New Forest

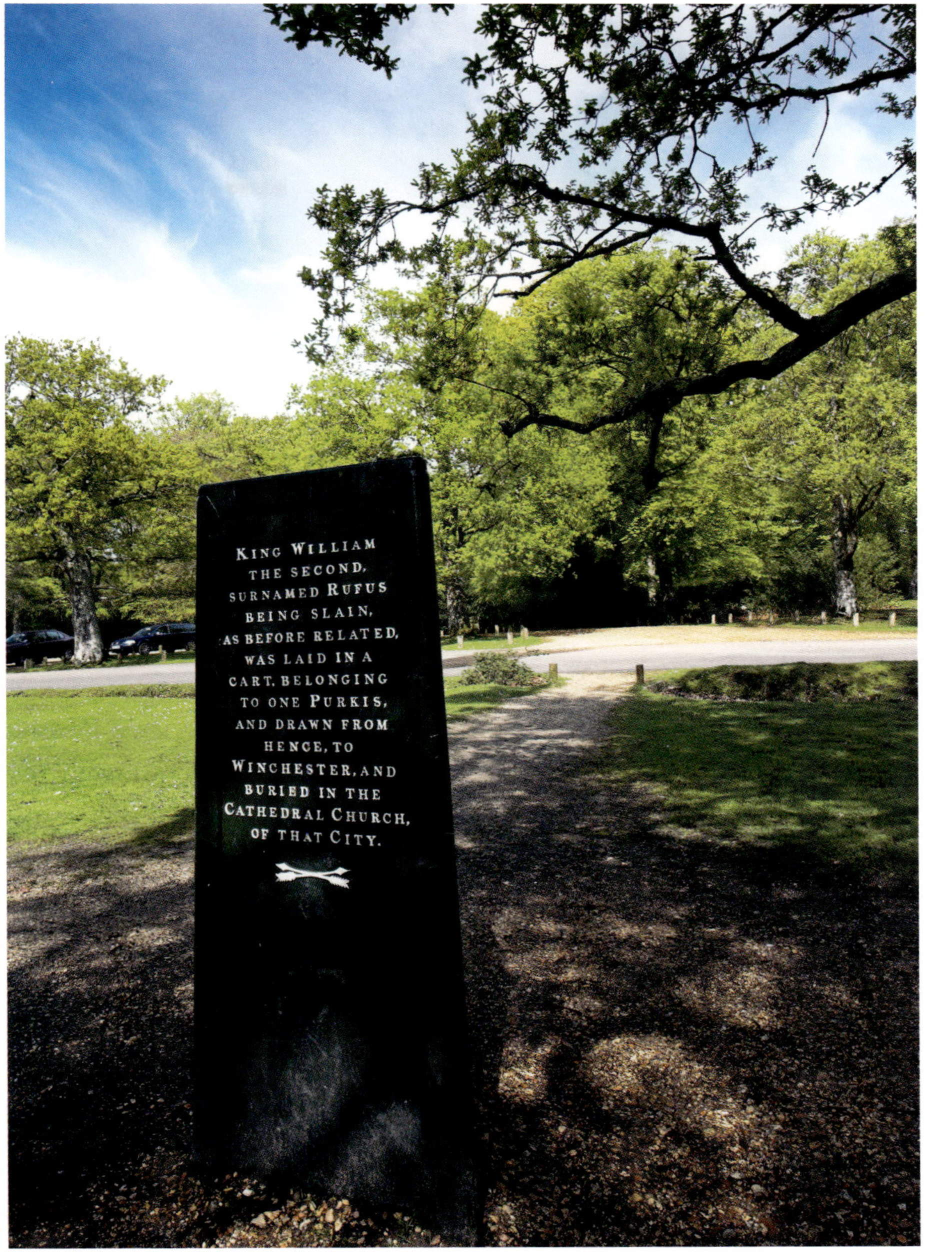

View of Rufus Stone where King William ll was killed by an arrow in the year 1100 while hunting at Stoney Cross in the New Forest

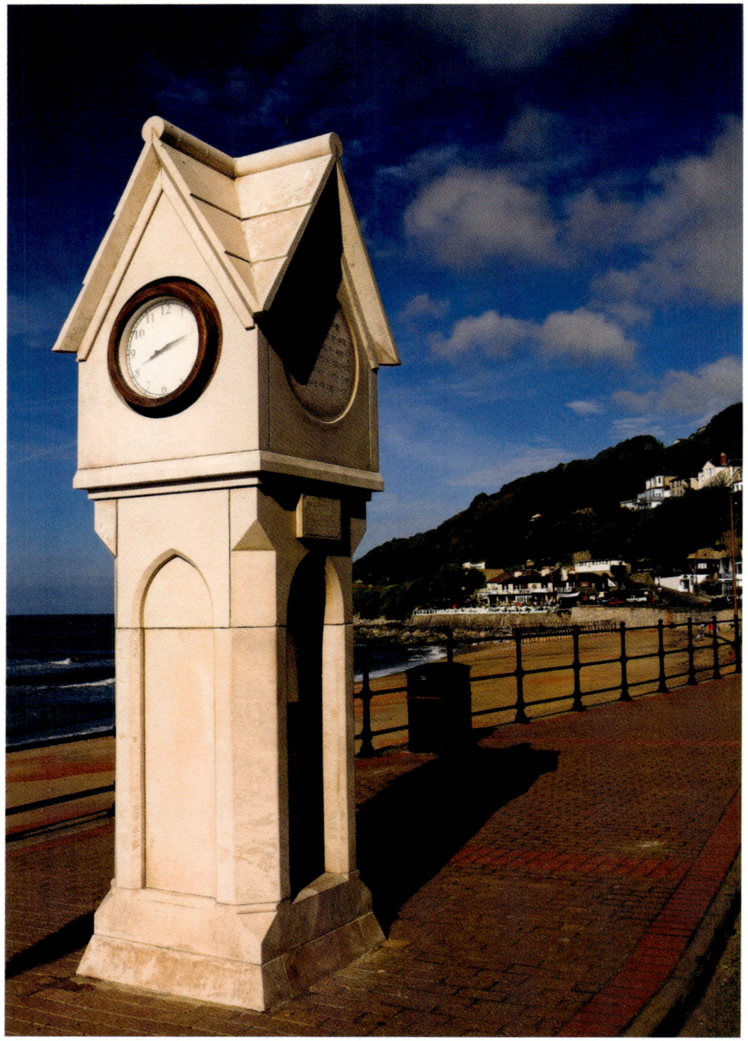

Ventnor esplanade and clock, Isle of Wight

Opposite: Deckchairs on the beach at Sandown set against the picturesque backdrop of Culver Cliffs, Isle of Wight

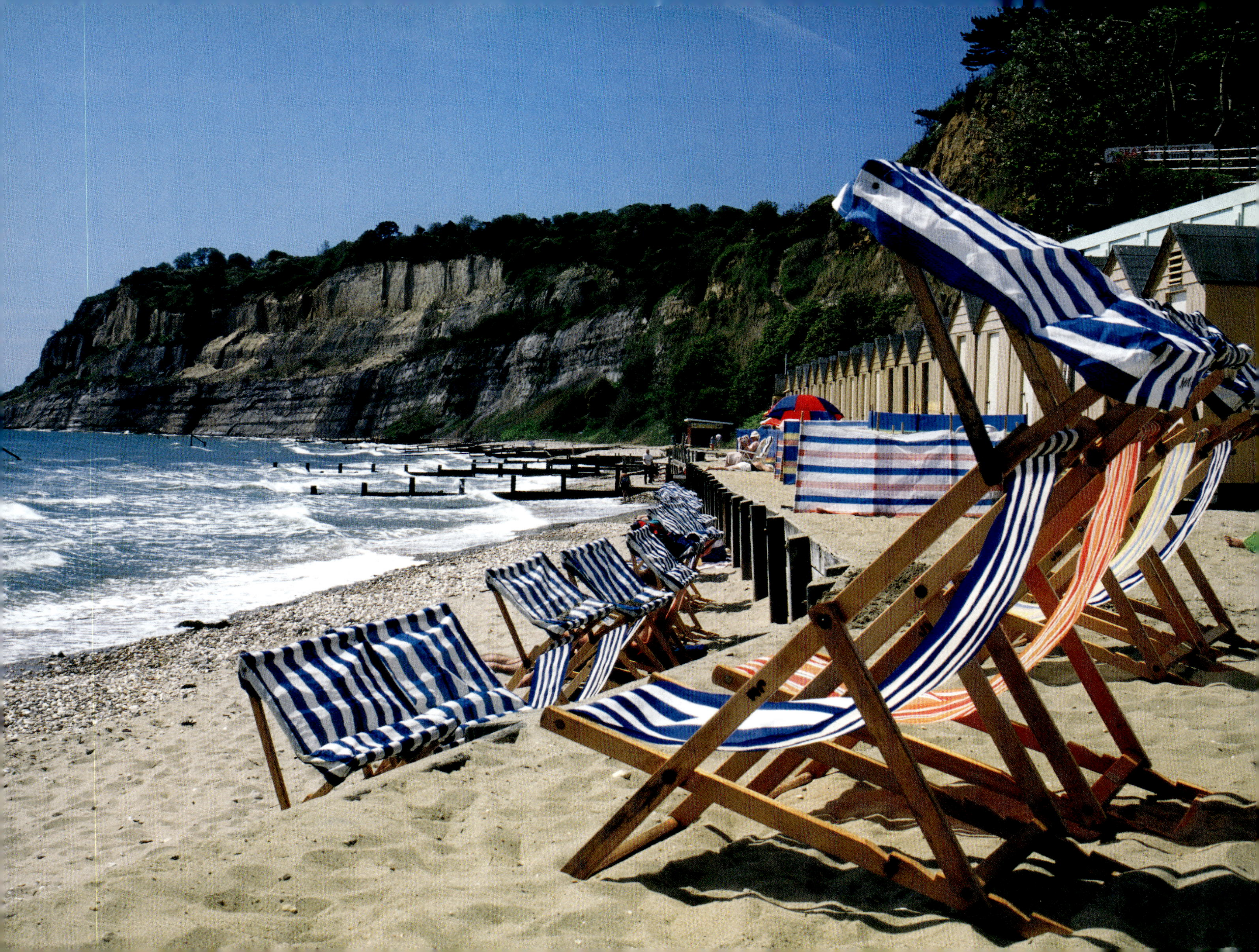

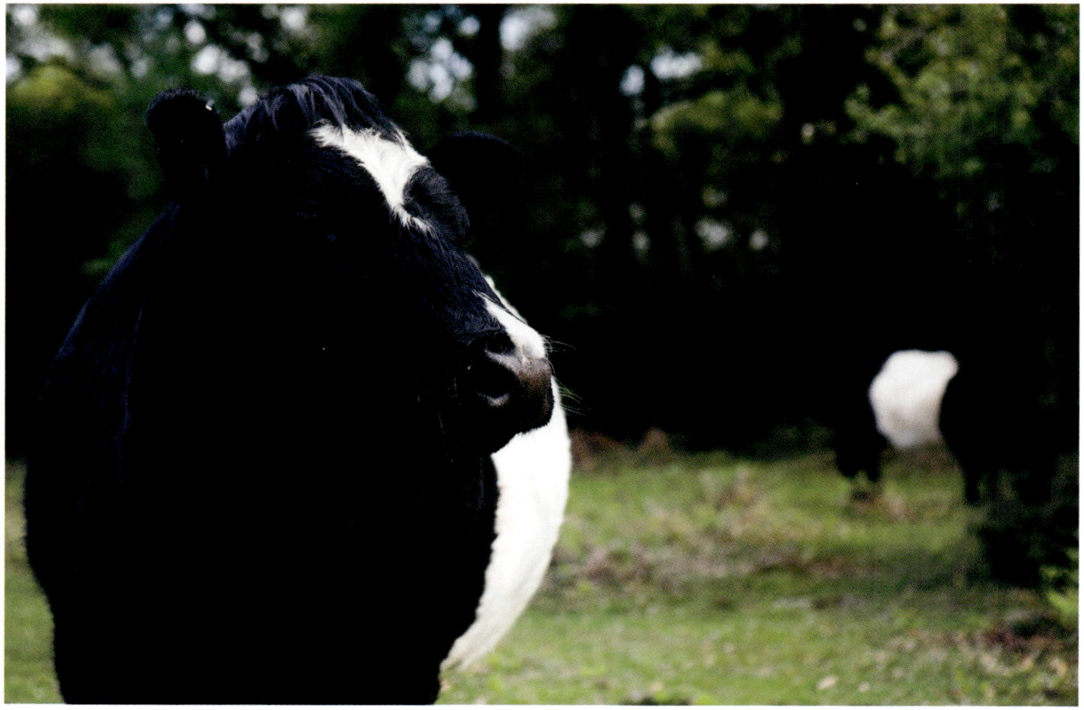

Belted Galloway cows grazing on Beaulieu heath, New Forest National Park

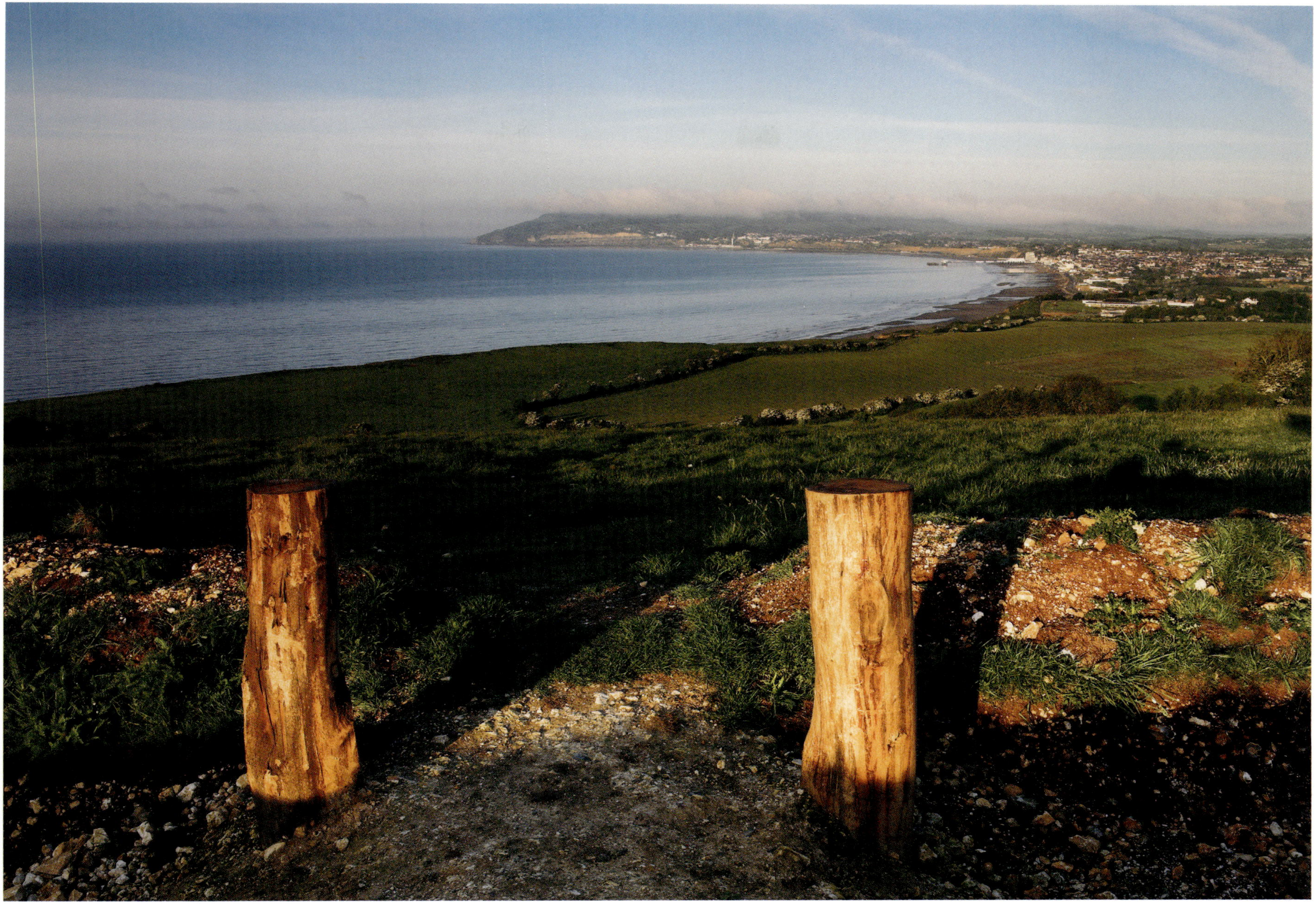

Early morning views over Sandown from Culver Down, Isle of Wight

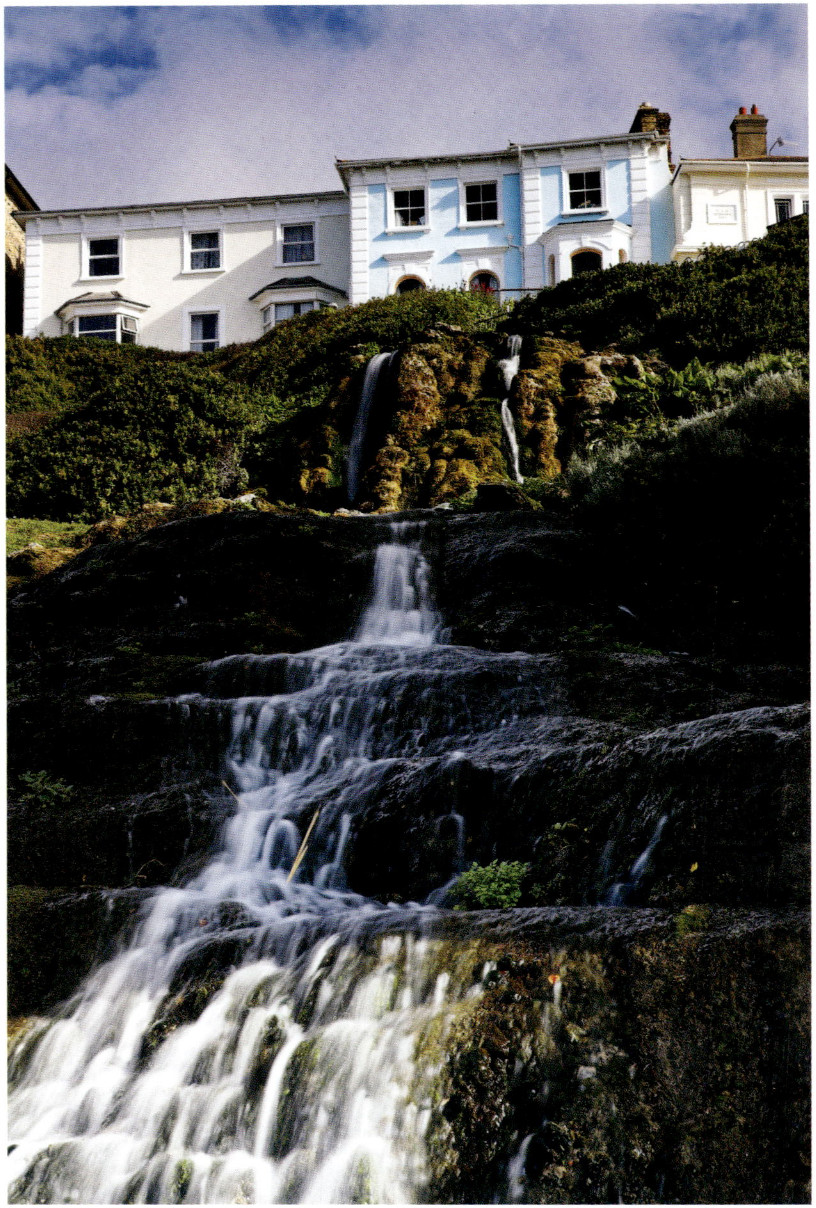

The waterfall at Cascade Gardens, Ventnor, Isle of Wight

Opposite: The famous Freshwater Bay viewpoint, showing the various chalk seastacks and Tennyson Down beyond

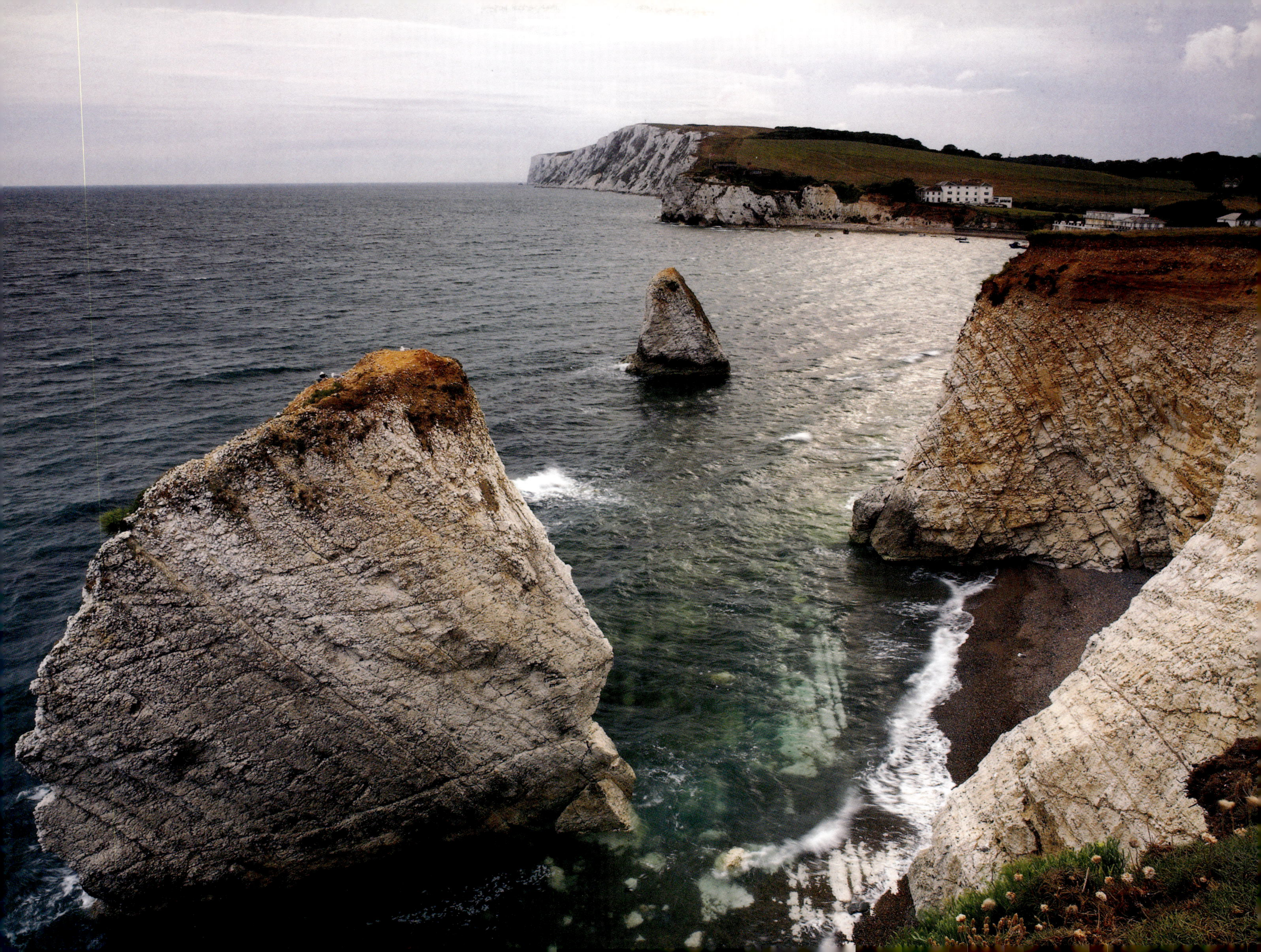

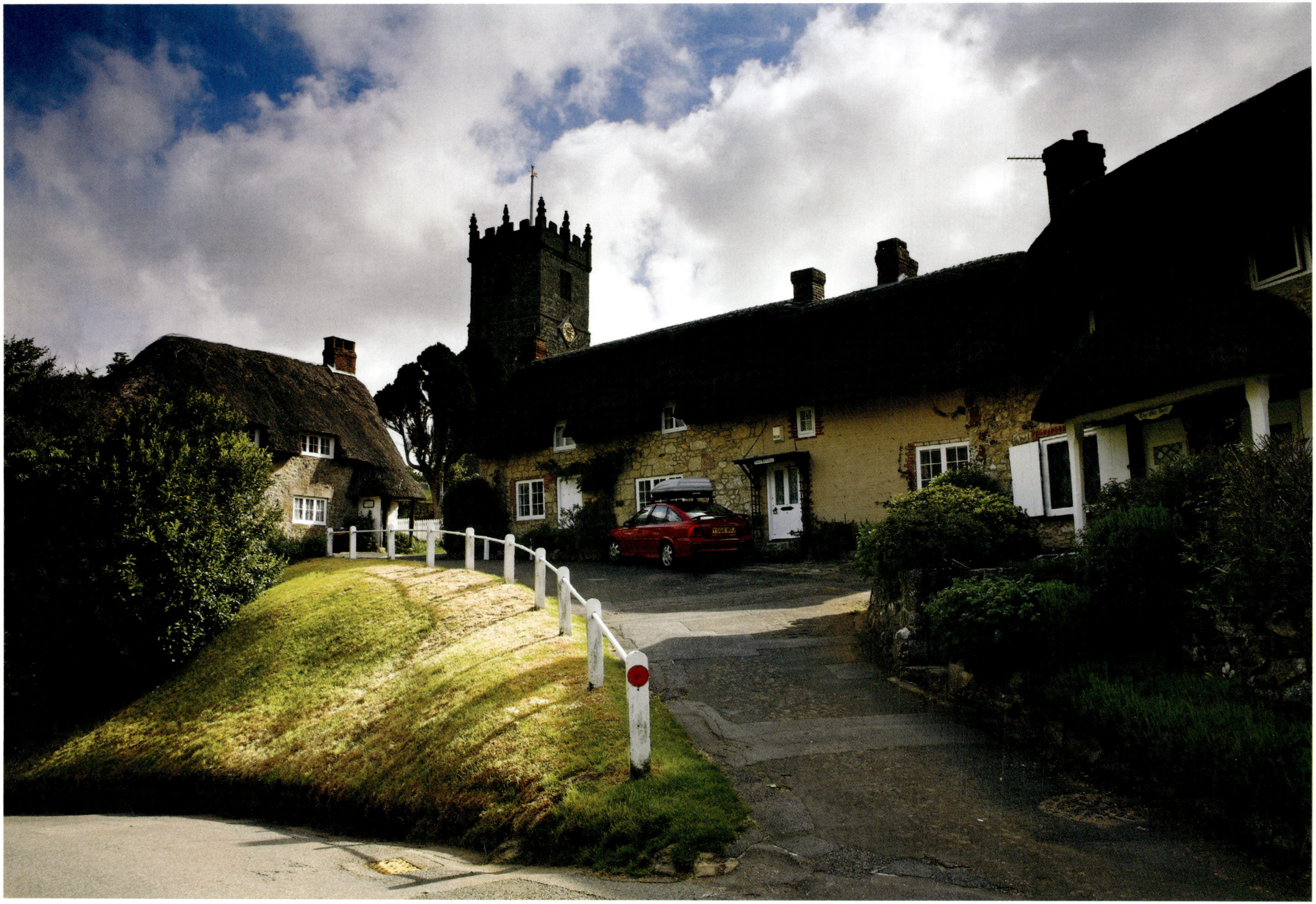

Thatched cottages leading up to Godshill church, Isle of Wight

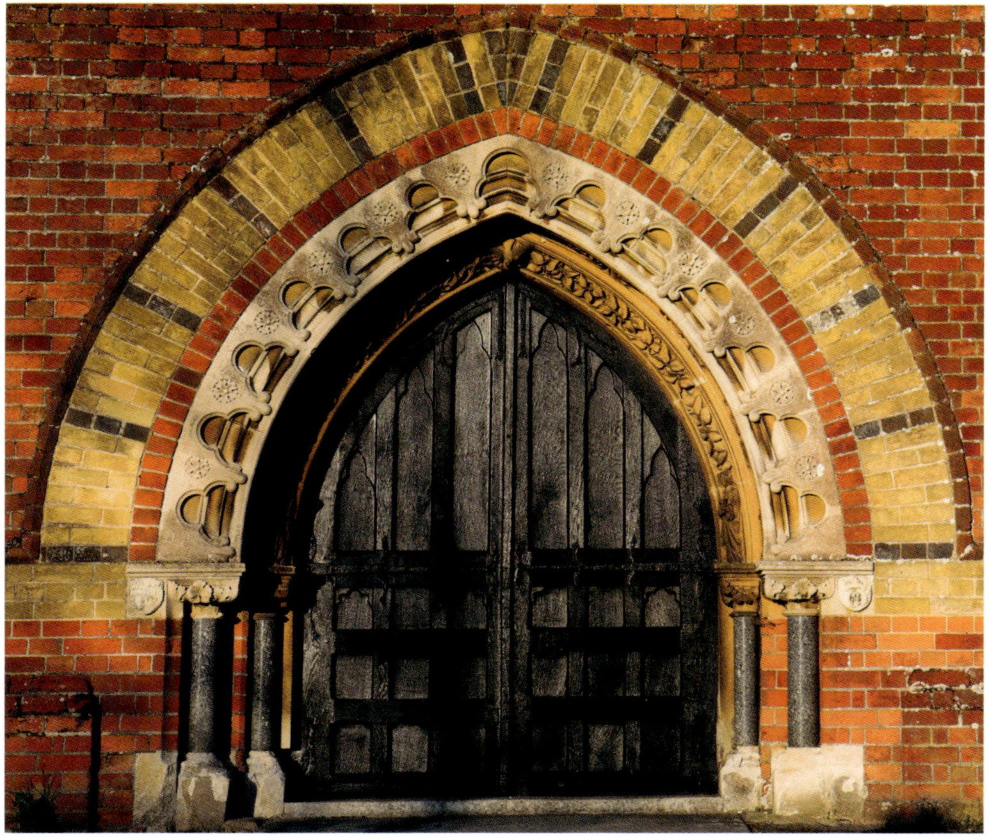

The ornate entrance to Lyndhurst Church, St Michael & All Angels in the New Forest. The grave of Alice Liddell, Lewis Carroll's inspiration for Alice in Wonderland, lies in the churchyard

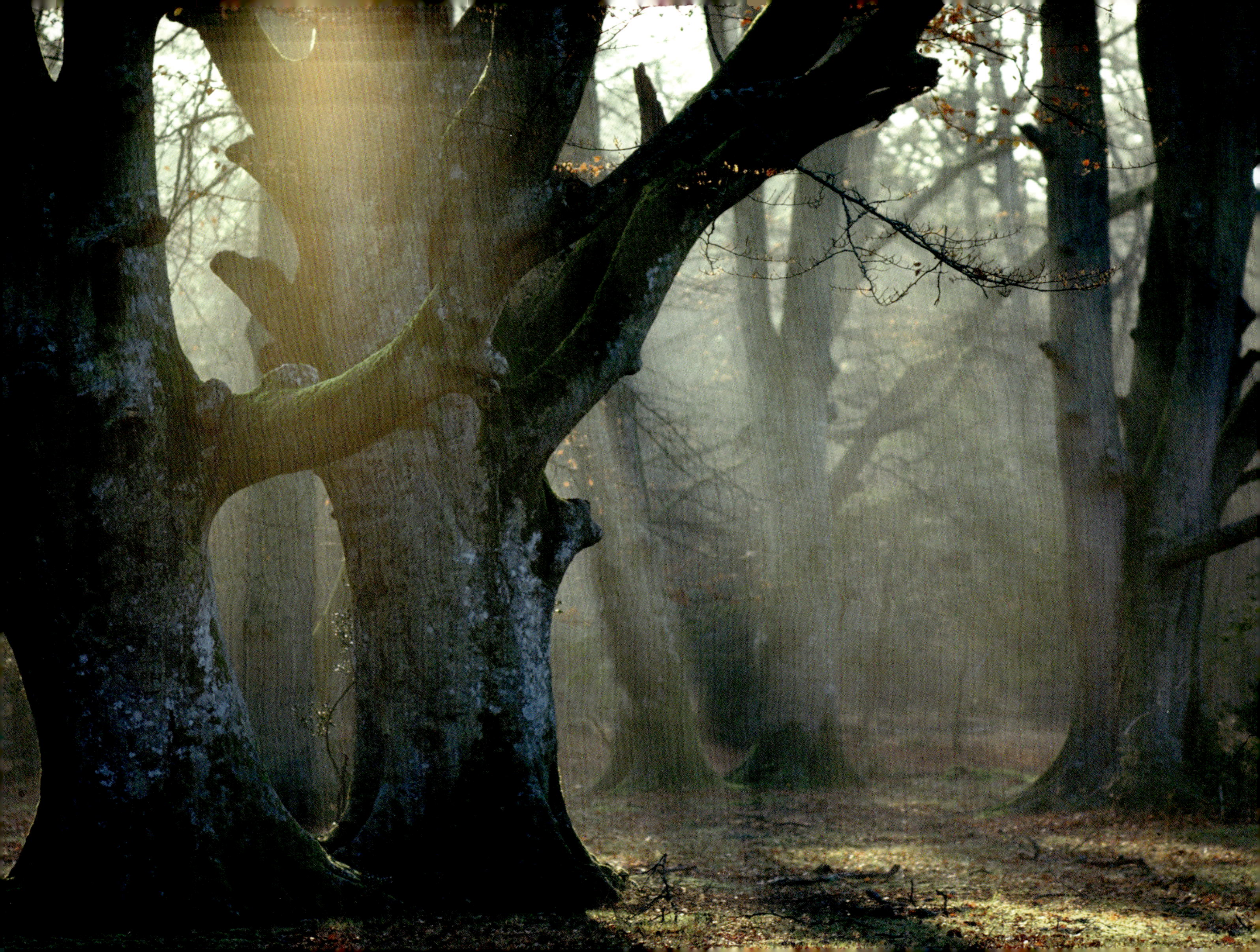

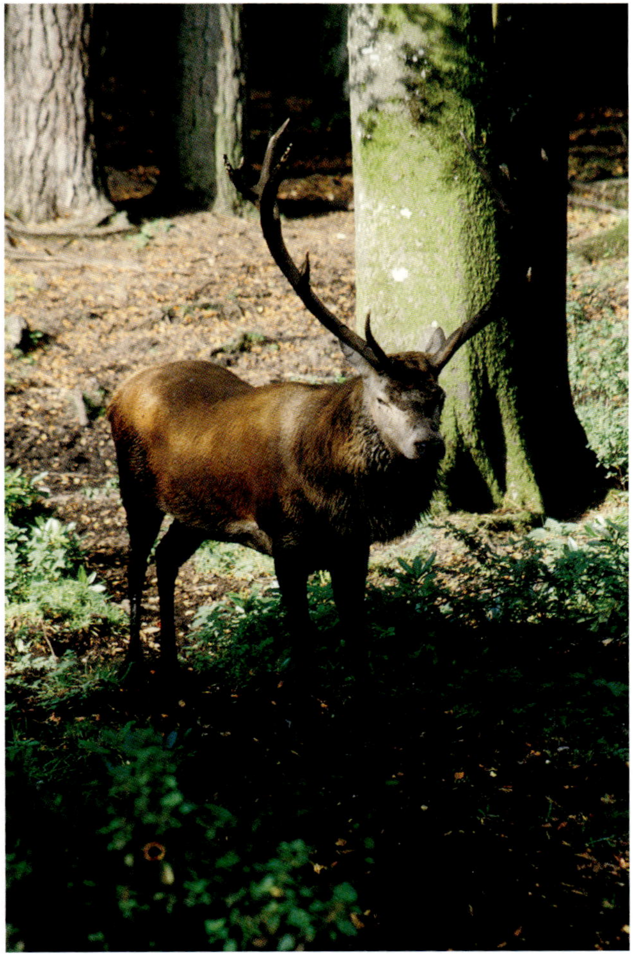

Red stag proudly displaying his antlers in the New Forest
Opposite: Mist and filtered sunlight in autumnal woodland, oak and beech glade near Bank in the New Forest

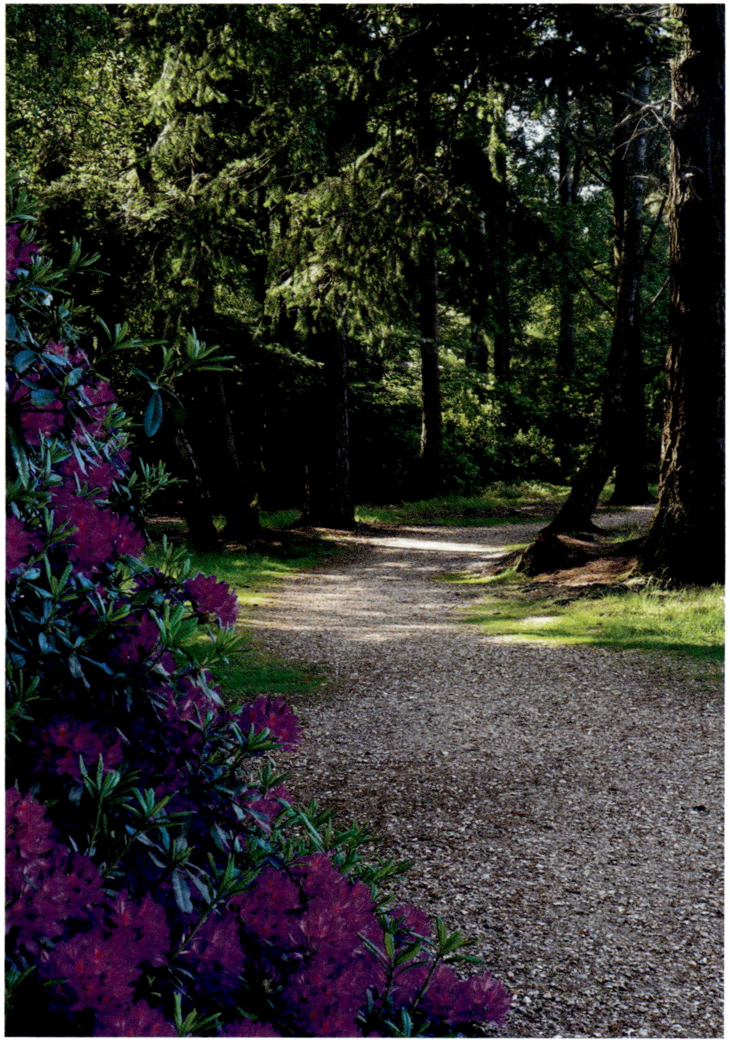

Rhododendrons on a pathway through the Rhinefield Ornamental Drive northwest of Brockenhurst, New Forest
Opposite: Ober Water meanders through the oak trees at Puttles Bridge, near Brockenhurst

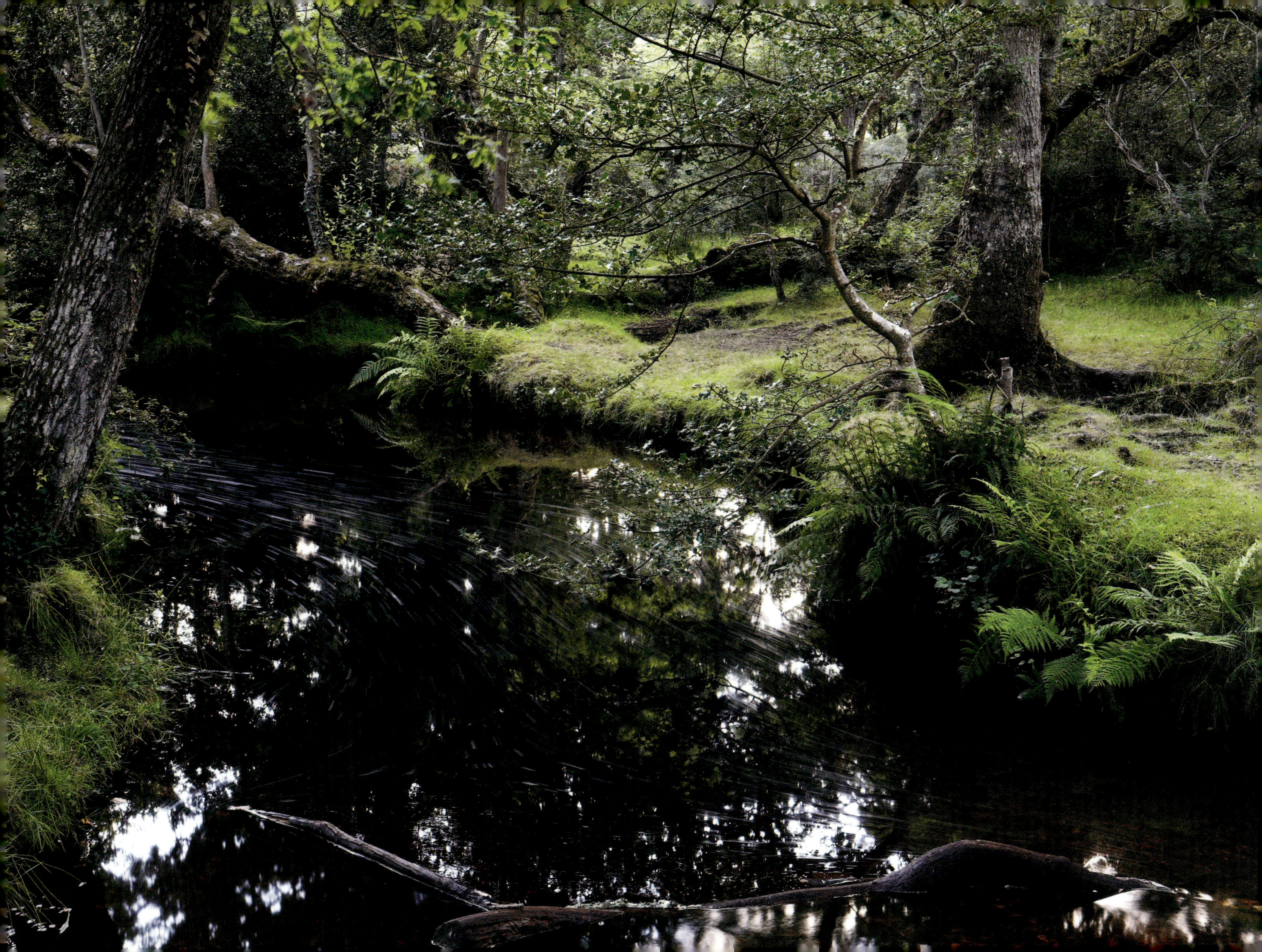

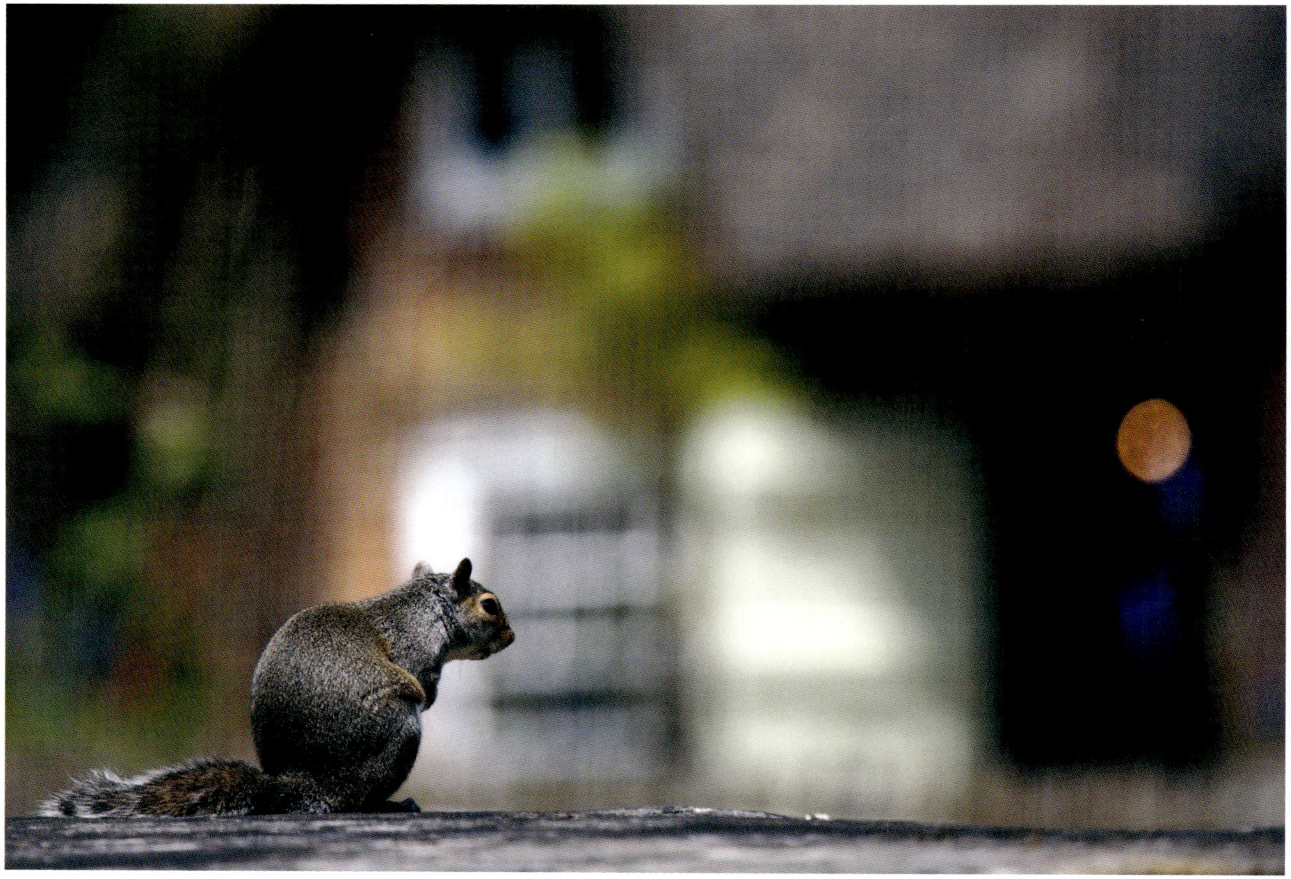

A grey squirrel in the New Forest

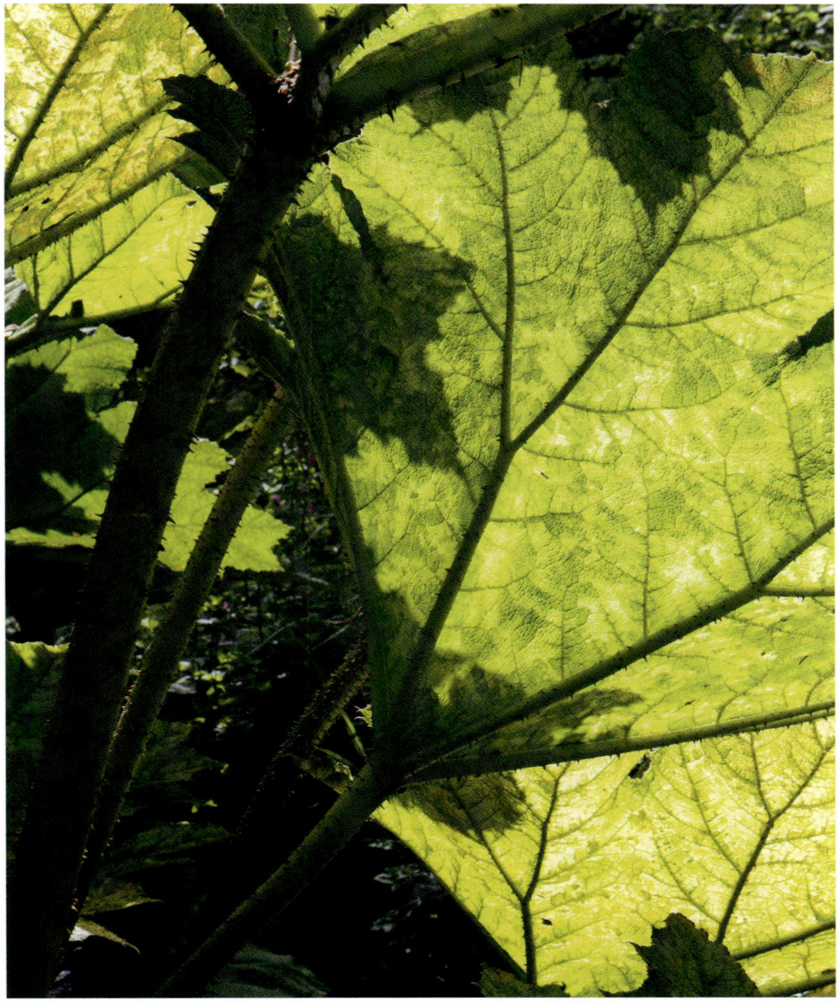

Sunlight illuminates the underside of the leaves of the gunnera plant, often known colloquially as 'giant rhubarb'

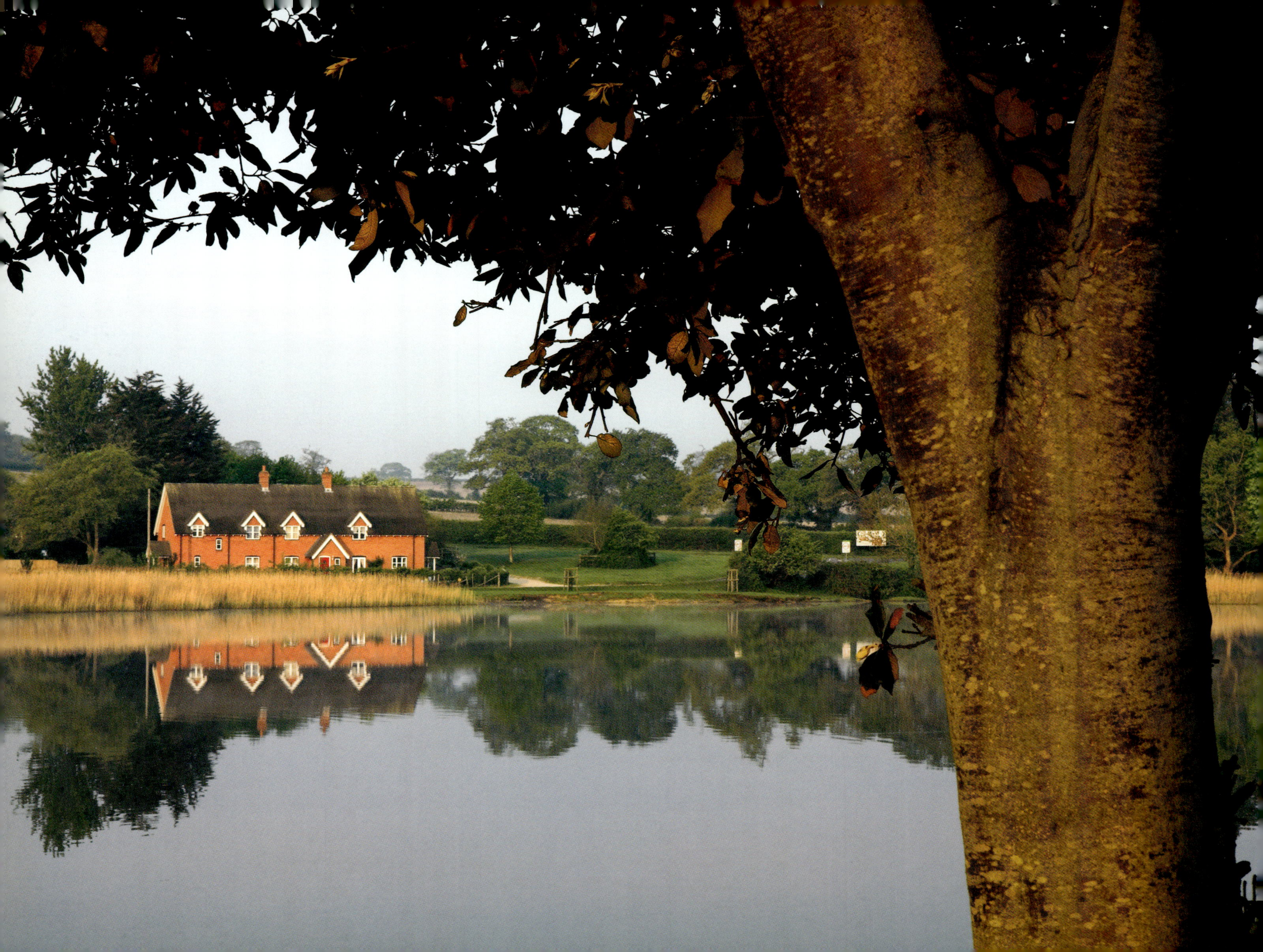

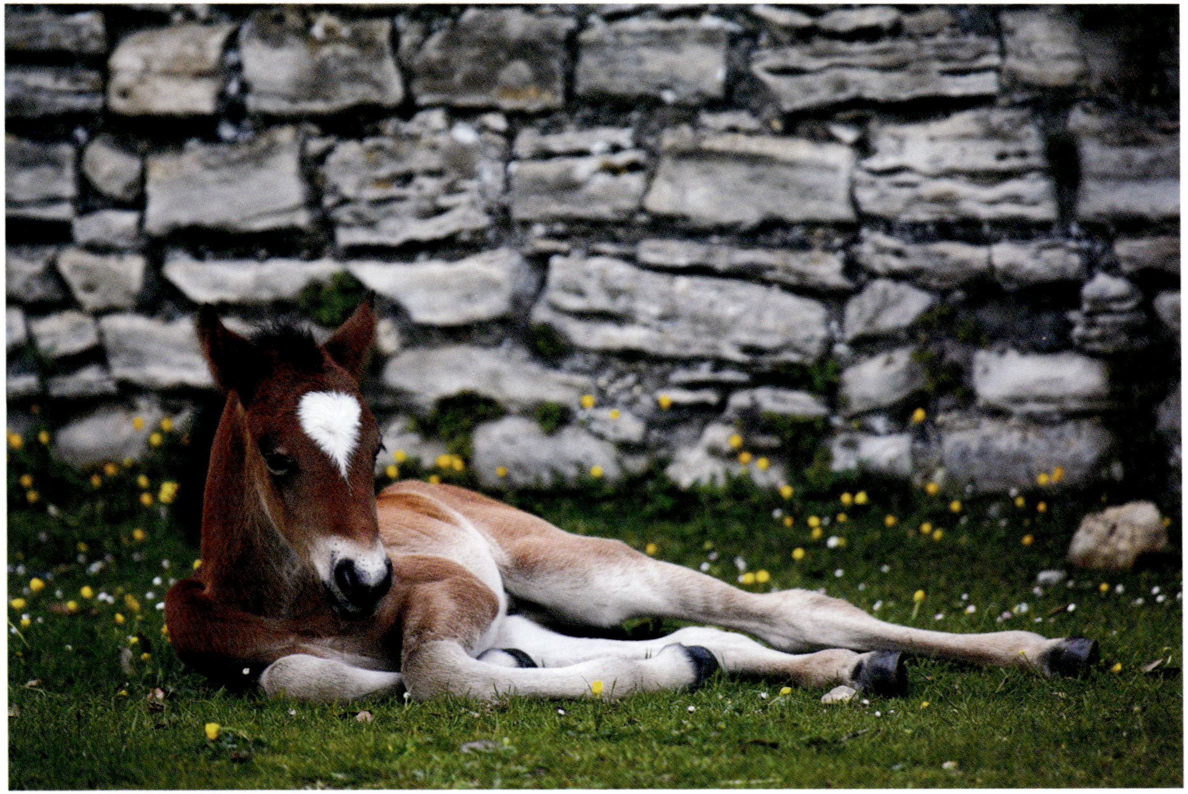

New Forest foal resting in Beaulieu village centre
Opposite: Cottages in Beaulieu village reflected in Beaulieu River

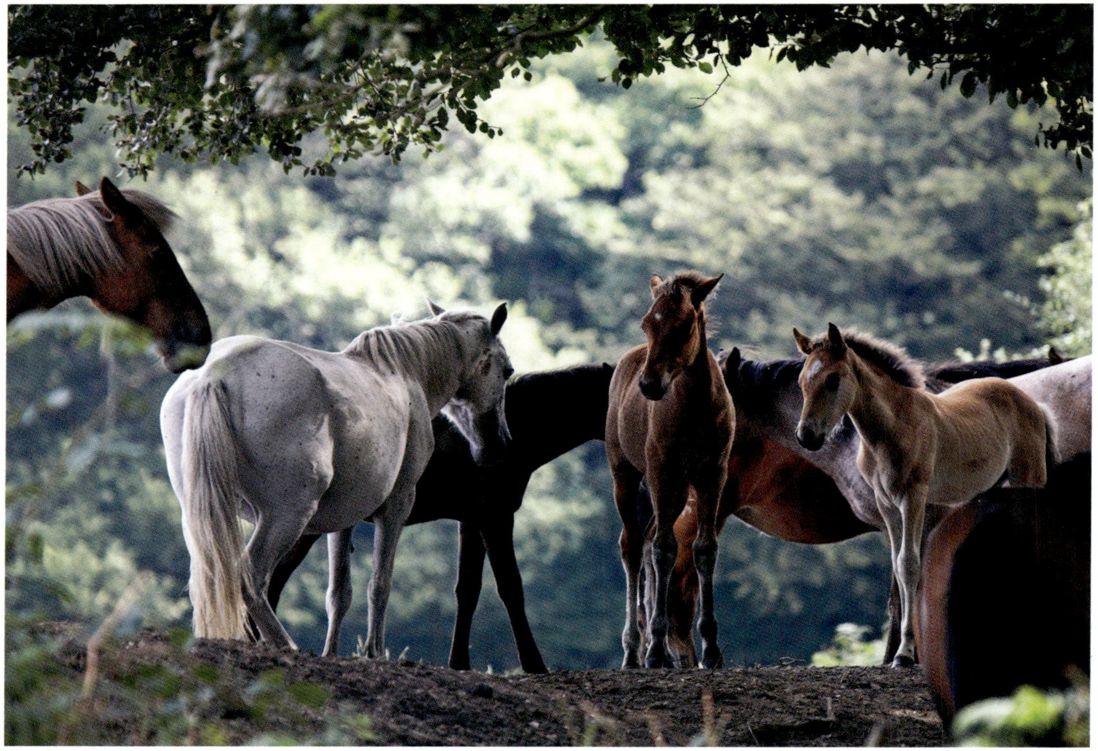

New Forest ponies seeking shade under the trees to escape the summer sun
Opposite: Scots pines glow in the golden evening light at Shatterford, near Marchwood in the New Forest

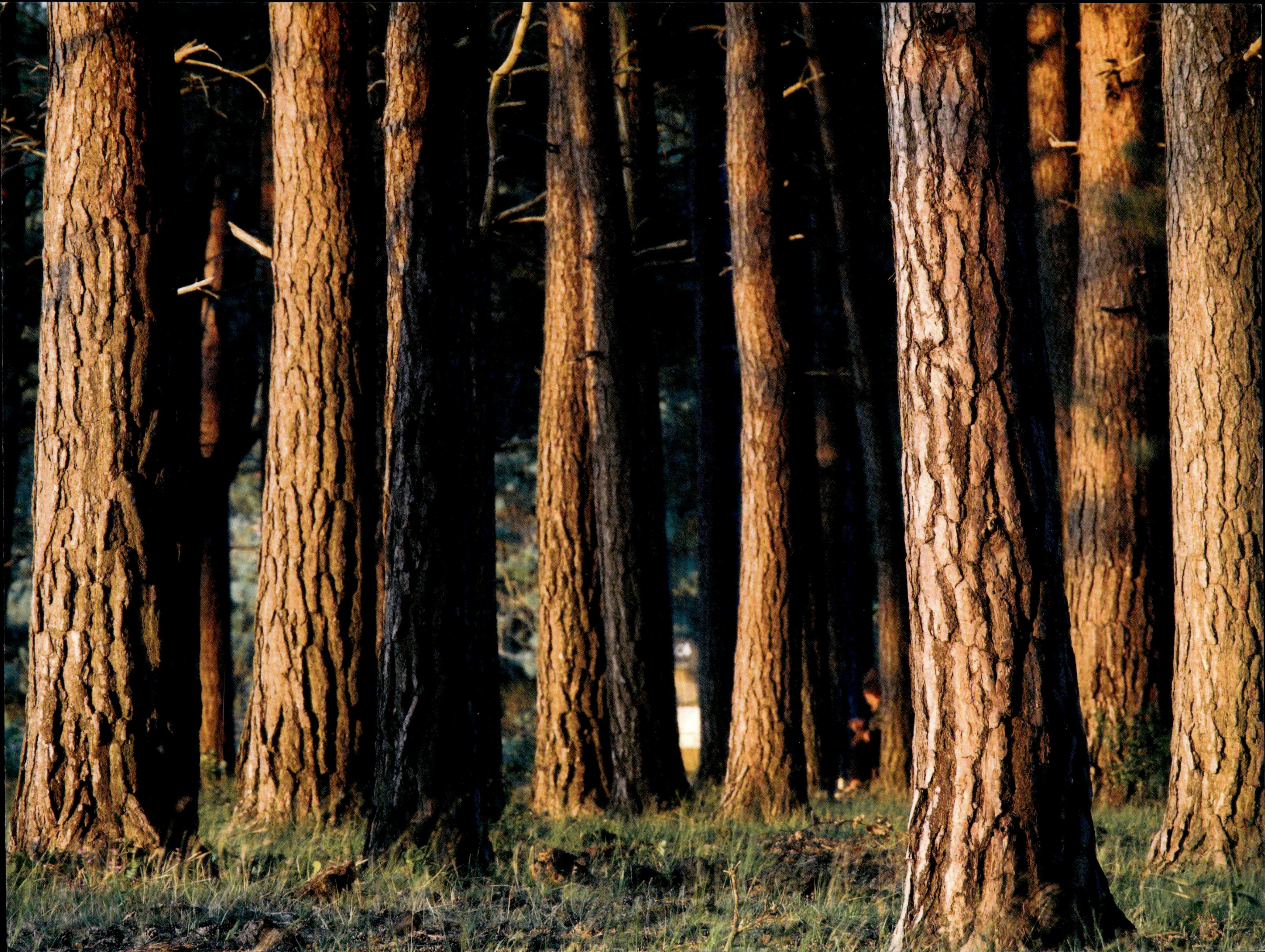

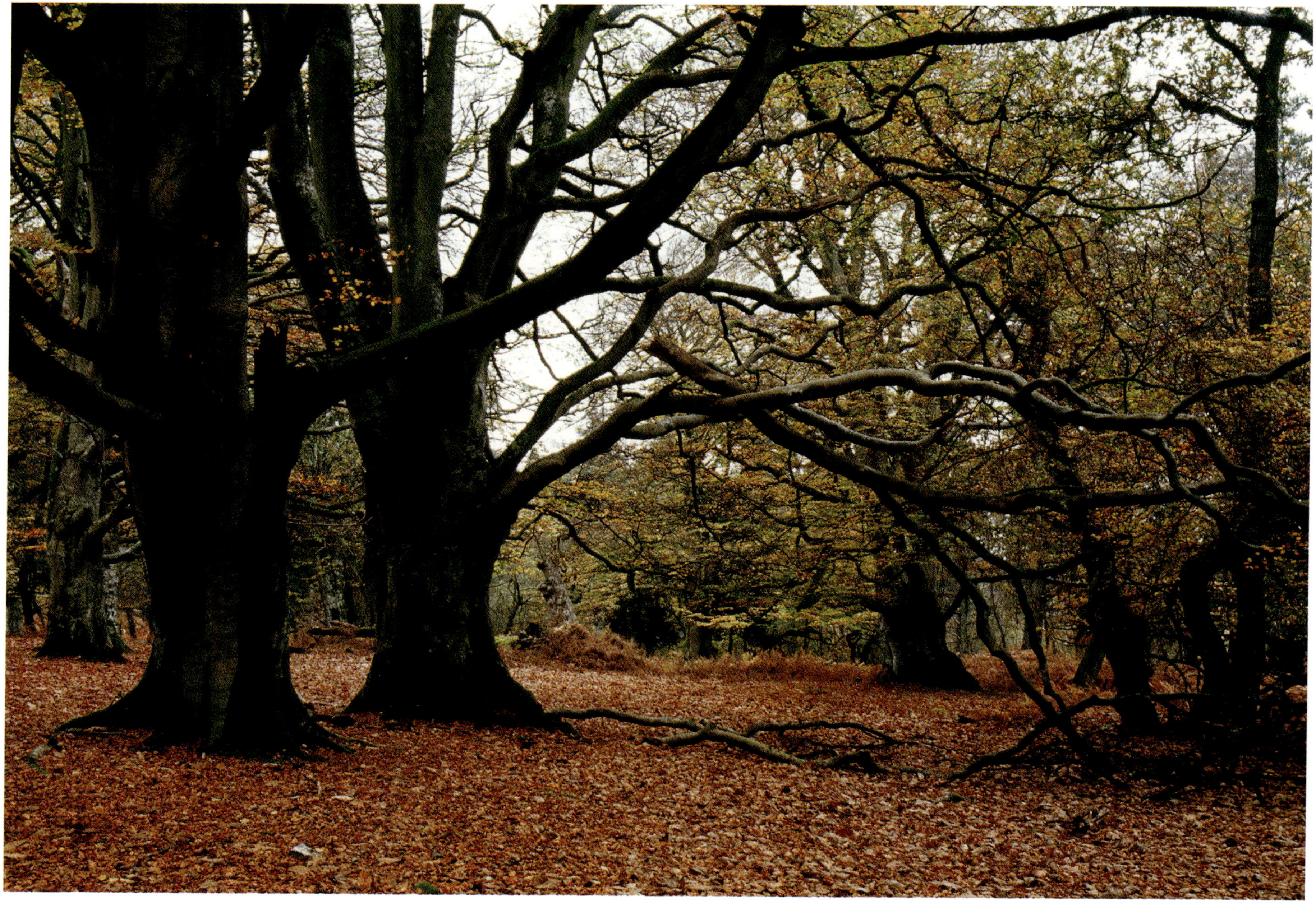

New Forest autumnal woodland scene
Opposite: Cliffs of Alum Bay at sunset on the Isle of Wight

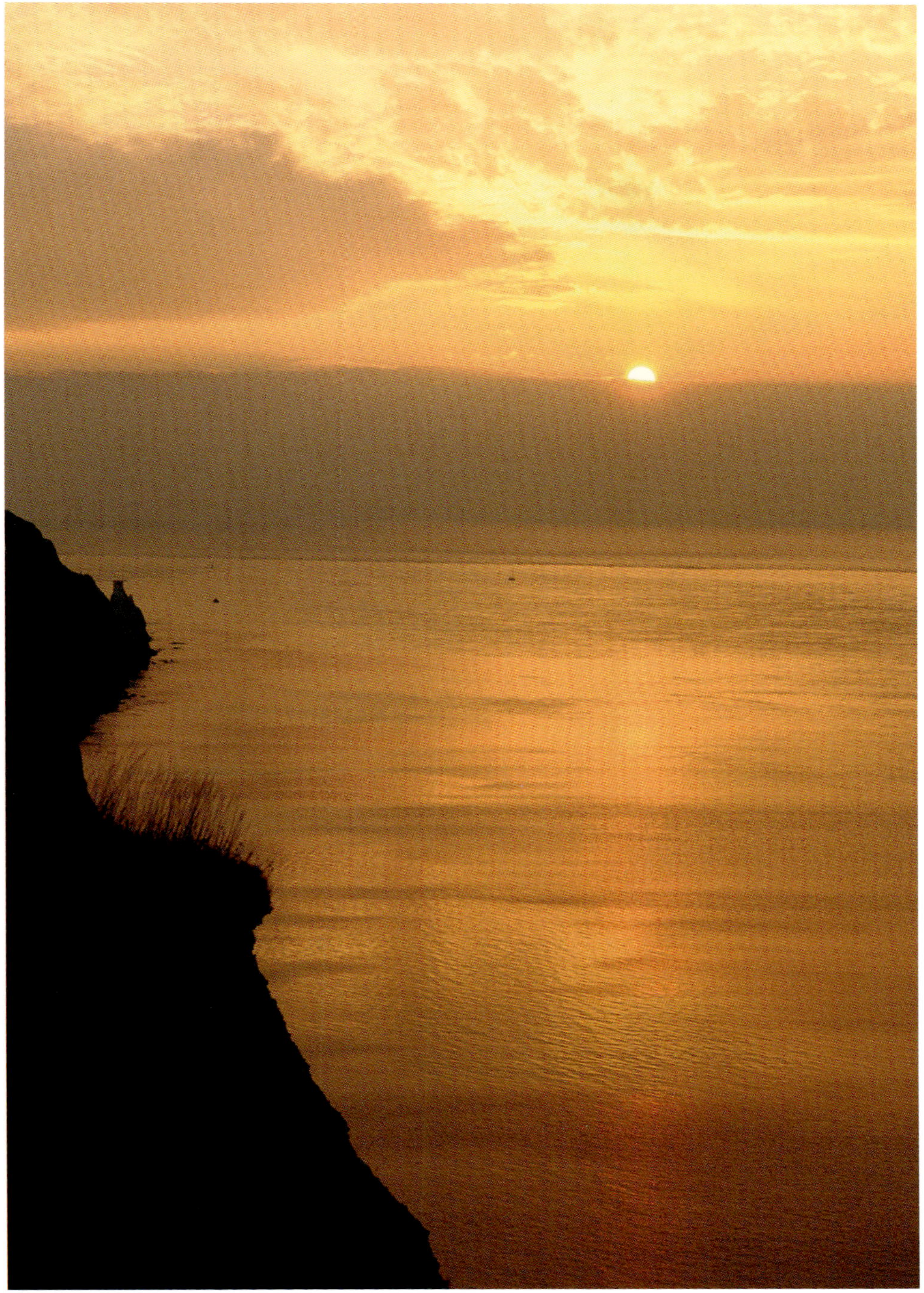

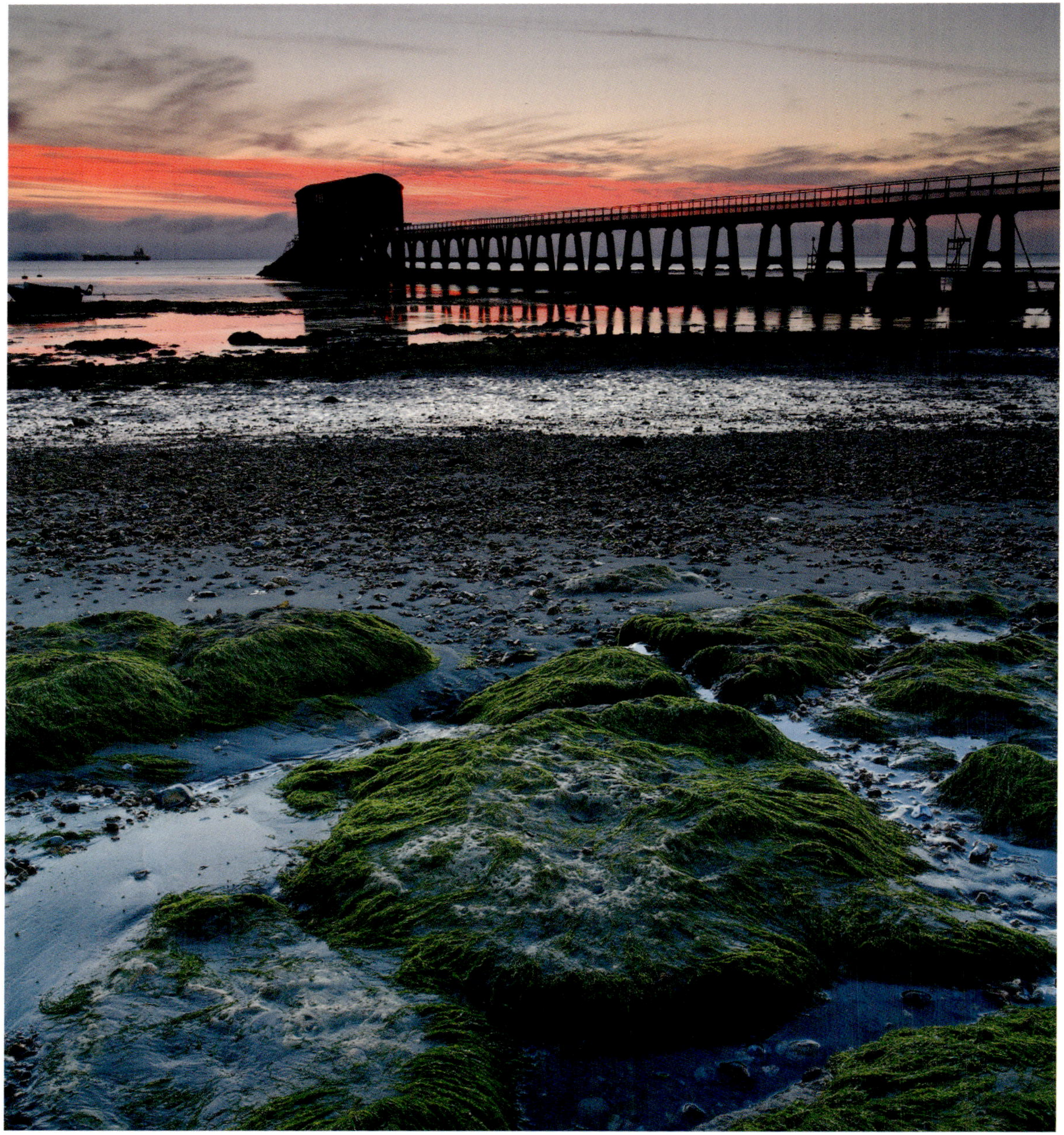

Pre-dawn glow over Bembridge Lifeboat pier, Isle of Wight

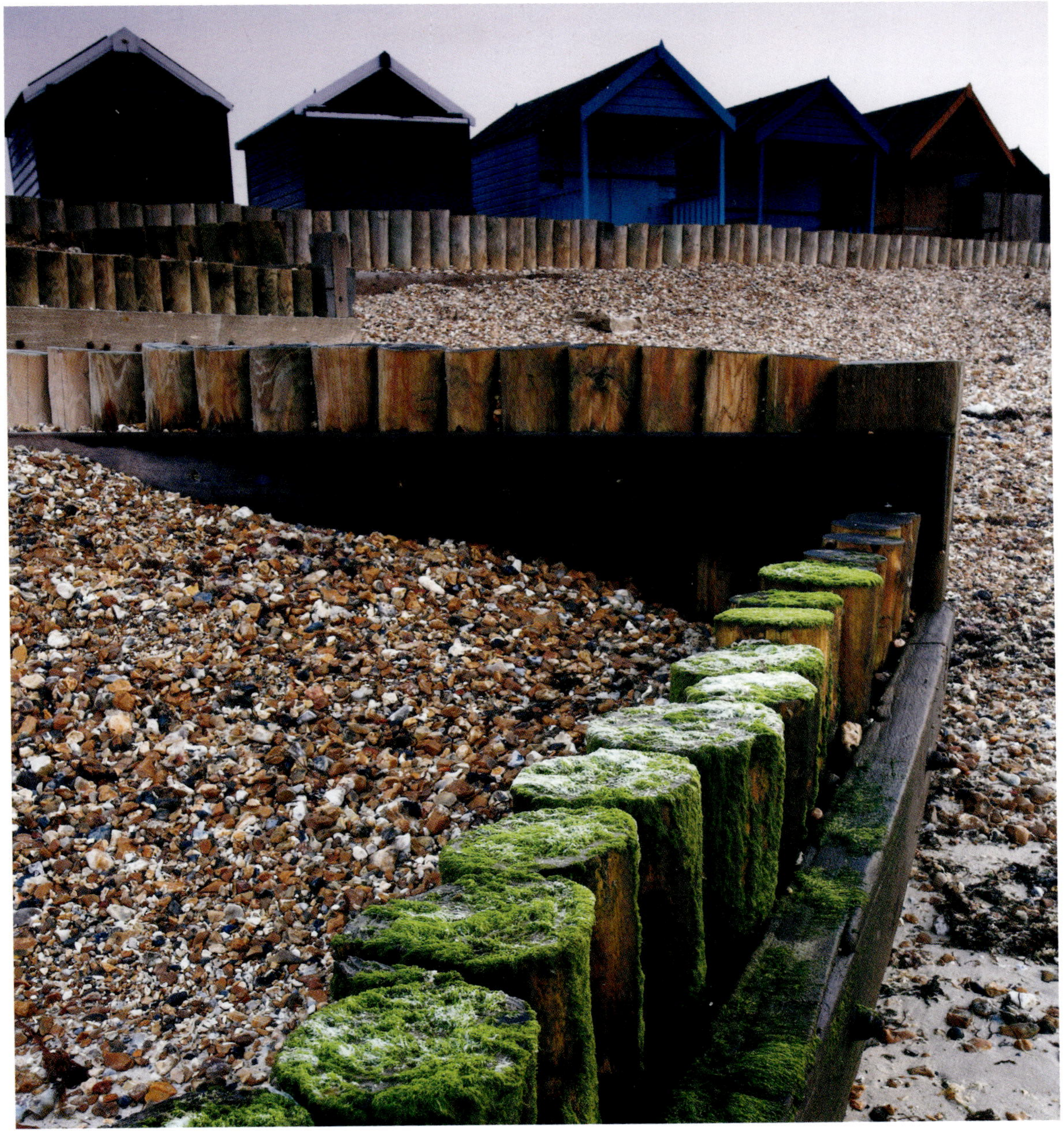

Seaweed-covered groynes leading up to beach huts at Calshot, Solent shore

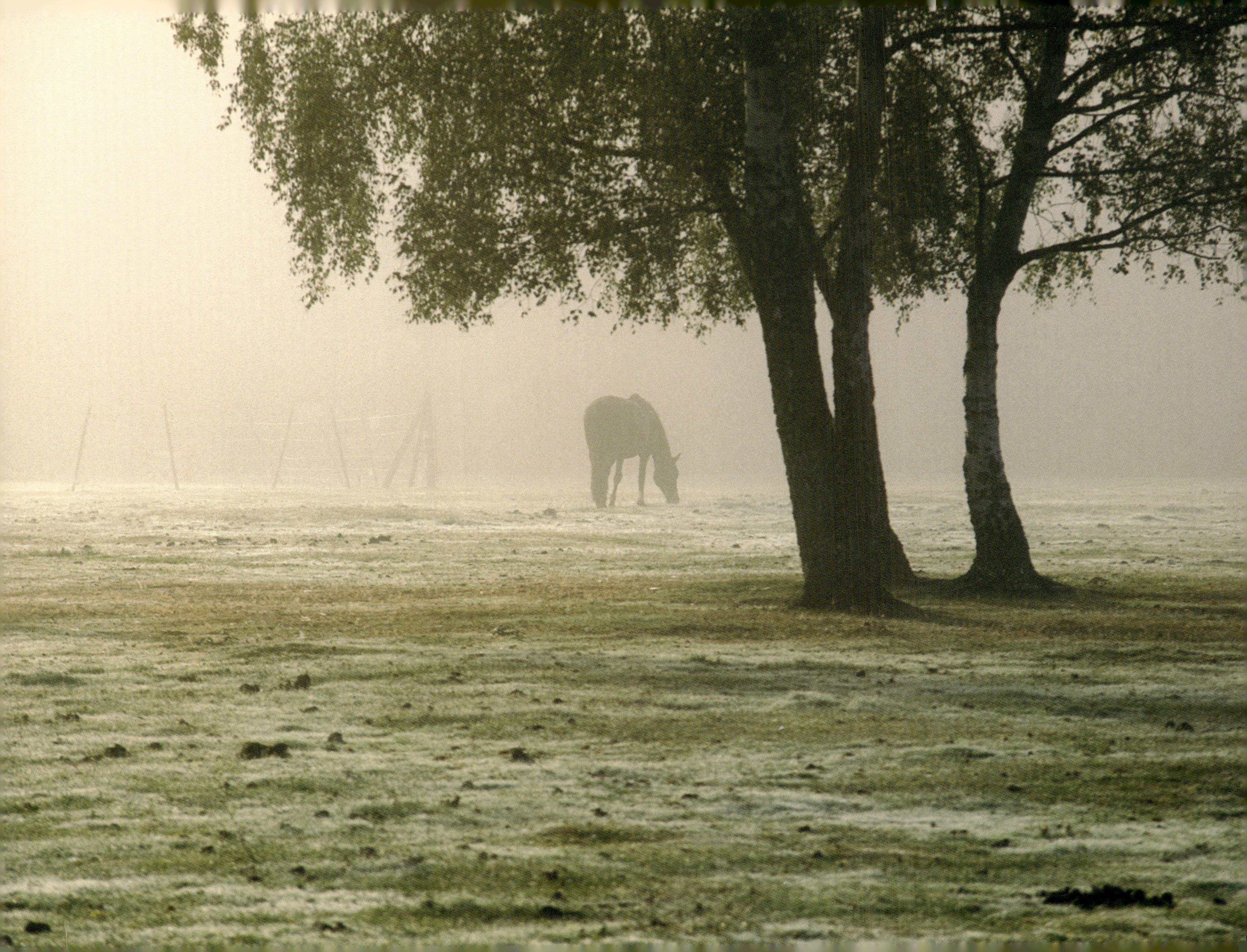

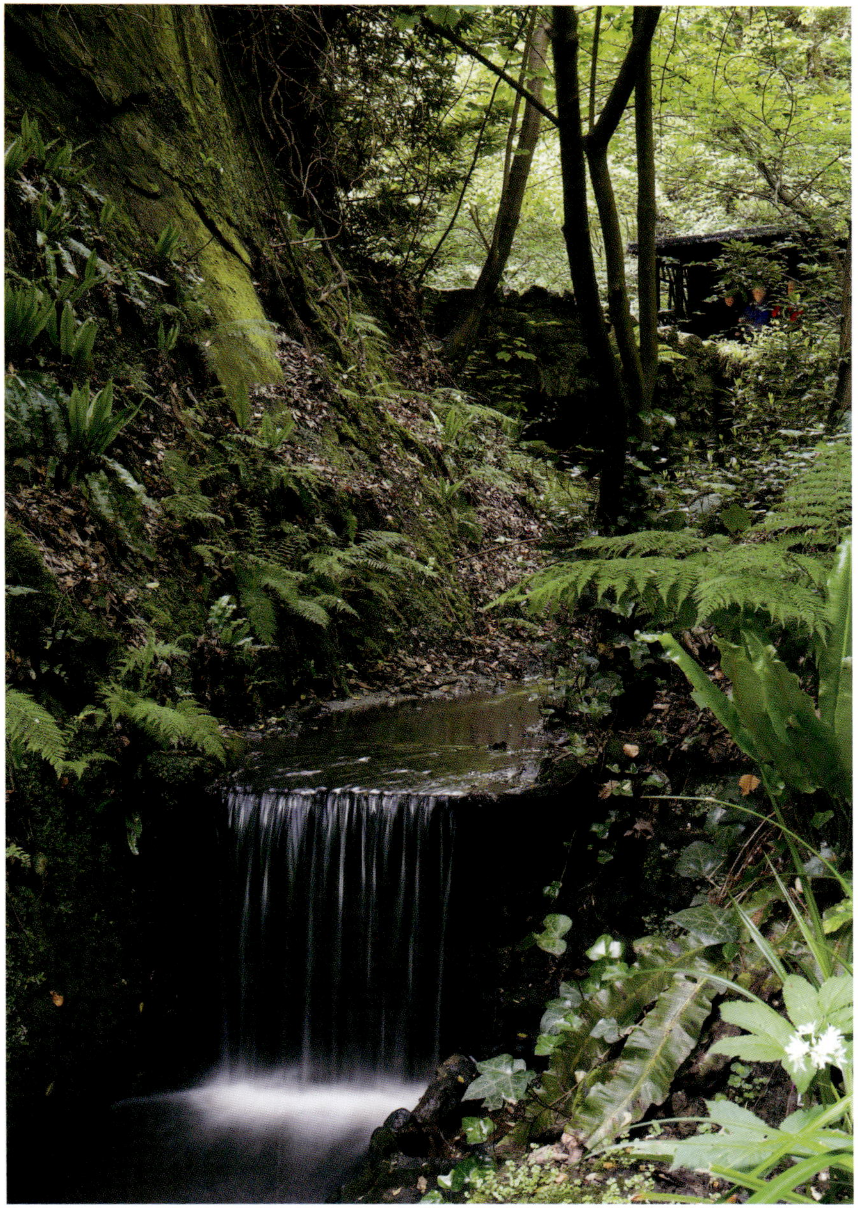

A small waterfall in Shanklin Chine, Isle of Wight
Opposite: New Forest pony silhouetted against early morning mists

INDEX